The Long Slow Death of
# Jack Kerouac

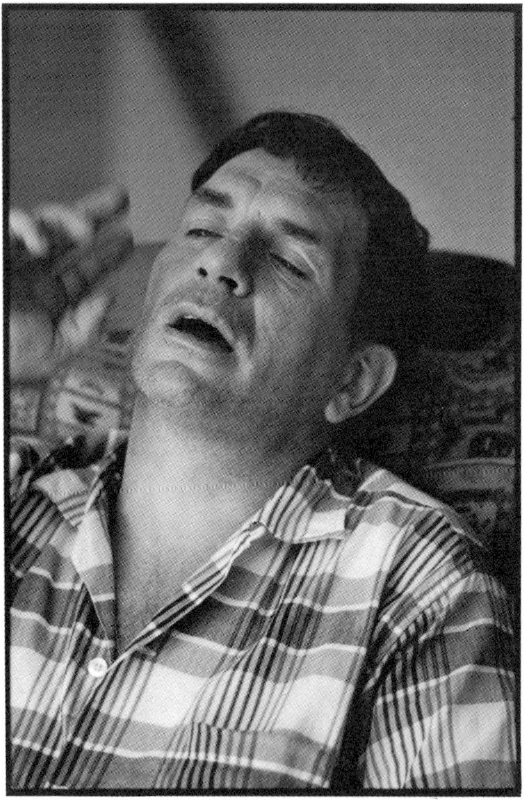

# The Long Slow Death of Jack Kerouac

*Jim Christy*

ECW PRESS

The publication of *The Long Slow Death of Jack Kerouac* has been generously supported by The Canada Council, the Ontario Arts Council, and the Government of Canada through the Book Publishing Industry Development Program.

Copyright © ECW PRESS, 1998

*All rights reserved.* No part of this publication may be reproduced, stored in a retrieval system, or transmitted in any form by any process — electronic, mechanical, photocopying, recording, or otherwise — without the prior written permission of the copyright owners and ECW PRESS.

SECOND PRINTING

CANADIAN CATALOGUING IN PUBLICATION DATA

Christy, Jim
The long slow death of Jack Kerouac
ISBN 1-55022-357-7

1. Kerouac, Jack, 1922–1969 — Last years.
2. Authors, American — 20th century — Biography.
3. Beat generation — Biography. I. Title.
PS3521.E735Z625 1998    813'.54    C98-931381-6

Cover and frontis photographs by Stanley Twardowicz.

Cover design by Guylaine Régimbald.

Imaging by ECW Type & Art, Oakville, Ontario.

Printed and bound by AGMV Marquis Imprimeur, Inc., Cap-Saint-Ignace, Québec.

Distributed in Canada by General Distribution Services, 325 Humber College Blvd., Etobicoke, Ontario M9W 7C3.

Distributed in the United States by LPC Group, 1436 West Randolph Street, Chicago, Illinois, U.S.A. 60607.

Distributed in the United Kingdom by Turnaround Publisher Services, Unit 3 Olympia Trading Estate, Coburg Road, Wood Green, London N2Z 6TZ.

Published by ECW PRESS,
2120 Queen Street East, Suite 200,
Toronto, Ontario M4E 1E2.

www.ecw.ca/press

PRINTED AND BOUND IN CANADA

"Take no thought beforehand what ye shall speak, neither do ye premeditate; but whatsoever shall be given to you in that hour, that speak ye, for it is not ye that speaks but the Holy Ghost!"
— Mark 13:11


"Life is fraught with imminent peril."
— W.C. Fields

# ONE

"Go thou across the land, go moan for man and of this world report you well and truly."
— Jack Kerouac, *On the Road*

There on the television screen a ribbon of highway unfolded through wild country and a voice intoned about The Road, that mad road of infinite possibilities. I was immediately aware of knowing the words, but for a moment couldn't recall from where. But only for a moment. I had, after all, been reading them for thirty-five years. It was the *context*. The car was no forty-nine Hudson, but a Volvo, for heaven's sake, an automobile associated with control and respectability, a car that wouldn't dare let you down. Neither would the fellow driving it; he certainly wasn't the type who'd leave you in fevers in Mexico City or go to the corner for cigarettes and call four days later from the coast or the drunk tank. No, he wasn't like the guy who wrote those words or the guy those words were written about. This citizen didn't need to pick up hillbilly hitchhikers for gas money, and if he wrecked that stodgy Swedish number down the winding mad road and went to meet his Maker, you can be damn sure they'd find more than sixty-two dollars in his bank account.

Not long before seeing that on the television, I'd noticed the same man's words used in an advertisement for Levi's jeans. And not long after seeing that on television, I read about a movie actor paying fifty thousand dollars for the dead author's raincoat and rain hat. There is a street named for him in San Francisco, a school in Colorado, and a monument of red granite in his hometown of Lowell, Massachusetts. But for those in charge of reputations — in North America, anyway — he's a joke. Loved or hated, he belongs now to the Ages, and the Ages don't know what the hell to make of him. Which isn't surprising, for it has ever been thus. Especially if you read his biographies.

# TWO

"She makes the scene. She reads Kerouac."
— Perry Como, "Like Young"

One bitter cold January evening in 1957, Joyce Glassman got a phone call from Jack Kerouac. They'd never met, but she knew about him and had, in her capacity as book editor, read his unpublished novel, *On the Road*. She'd also seen the picture of him in *Mademoiselle* that had accompanied an article about the emerging Beat Generation. Allen Ginsberg had told her about Kerouac and all his other buddies. Kerouac asked Joyce if she cared to meet him at the Howard Johnson's on Eighth Street. She agreed, took the subway downtown, got off at Astor Place, and walked across town with trepidation. She had on a red coat, was twenty-one, "round-faced and blonde."

Jack had told her he had black hair and would be sitting at the counter, wearing a black-and-red-checked shirt. She approached him shyly. He didn't have any money, so she bought him dinner — frankfurters, home fries, and beans — and the whole time he's eating, she's stealing looks at him "because he's beautiful. You're not supposed to say a man is beautiful, but he is."

They left together, walked to the subway underneath

an airline sign that suggested, "Fly Now, Pay Later," rode up to Joyce's two-room apartment near Columbia and the West End Bar. Kerouac moved in or, rather, stayed with Joyce between trips to Europe, or California, or his mother's house in Orlando, Florida.

Kerouac was in Orlando on September 3, 1957, when he boarded a Greyhound bound for New York, where *On the Road*, a book he'd written six years earlier, was being published on the fifth. All the afternoon of the fourth, Joyce stood at the window of her new place on Sixty-Eighth Street waiting for him. He'd written her, "I can hardly wait to hold you in my arms."

Somewhere around midnight, they woke groggy from "the blacked-out sleep that comes after making love," threw on their clothes, and went out to the newsstand on Sixty-Sixth Street. There was supposed to be a review of *On the Road* in the *Sunday Times*.

There was, and neither of them had ever read a review like it. Written by Gilbert Millstein, it had all the weight of a pronouncement for the ages: "*On the Road* is the second novel by Jack Kerouac, and its publication is a historical occasion insofar as the exposure of an authentic work of art is of any great moment in an age in which the attention is fragmented by the superlatives of fashion (multiplied a millionfold by the spirit and power of communication.)"

They went to Donnelly's bar and read the thing over and over. Here was Jack Kerouac, thirty-five years old, "beautiful," and "the principal avatar" of an entire generation. He had already written several other books, enough anyway upon which to lay legitimate claim to being the greatest writer of his age. Furthermore, he was about to have money for the first time in his life. The world was laid out before him.

Yet Jack was perplexed. He kept shaking his head. Joyce was frightened. Perhaps they knew what awaited. But how could they? No writer of his generation had as much experience of the world as Jack Kerouac, but there was no precedent in history for what that review presaged. If the bitch goddess Fame, and Myth, her bastard brother, wanted to slay the most susceptible person, chew him up and spit out the pieces, they picked the right guy.

Jack and Joyce went up the stairs for a few hours' sleep before began the onslaught they never dreamed. Or at least Joyce climbed the stairs with the corporeal Jack. The other Jack never went up. Jack Kerouac was already gone, real gone.

# THREE

"O pitiful, lovable, soon-to-be departed earth —"
— Jack Kerouac, *Visions of Gerard*

His life started with a mistake. The priest at St. Louis de France entered his name in the church registry as Jean-Louis Kerouac. He was born on March 12, 1922, at 9 Lupine Road in the Little Canada section of Lowell, Massachusetts.

Ancestors on his father's side had come to Quebec to fight for France on the Plains of Abraham. His grandfather, Jean-Baptiste Kirouack, was a potato farmer in Rivière du Loup, Quebec, who married Clémentine Bernier. Kerouac's father, born in Rivière du Loup, was Joseph Alcide Léon Kirouack, called Leo. He had two brothers and a sister. Of the two boys, one was a cripple, the other a lunatic; the sister became a prostitute.

At the turn of the century, nearly three million left a land of no jobs and small, unproductive farms for the mills and factories of New England. There was a joke in the new land that when one of these large French-Canadian families stepped down from the train, the local population doubled.

Jean-Baptiste's family was one that made this exodus, arriving in Nashua, New Hampshire, in 1902. It is said his death a few years later was the result of drinking too much whiskey blanc, a vodka-like homebrew made from potato peelings.

Young Leo, handsome, black-haired, blue-eyed, and ambitious, became an apprentice printer and wrote articles for a French newspaper in Nashua. He moved to Lowell to serve as jack-of-all-trades on *L'Etoile*, a newspaper his boss had purchased. For a mate, Leo chose Gabrielle L'Evesque, an orphan who had toiled in shoe factories since she was a small child and had never been out of Nashua.

Their first child, Francis Gerard, was born in 1916; a daughter, Caroline, in 1918; Jean-Louis, the last child, four years later. Jean-Louis was a fat baby, called Ti-Pousse — Little Thumb — by his father. His earliest memories were of Gerard and the haunting iconography of the Catholic church. He saw processions of black-clad nuns out the window. His brother took him through the stations of the cross at the side of the nearby church. There were crucifixes, palm-frond crosses, and replicas of bleeding hearts throughout the Kirouack household. Gerard was kind to animals, told his little brother about saints and angels, interpreted his own dreams, and made up stories that combined all the elements. It wasn't the official religion but a sort of French-Canadian holy folklore.

Gerard died of rheumatic fever in 1926, when he was nine years old. It was, and would always remain, the most significant event in Jean-Louis' life. His brother had taught him the holiness of life, the possibility of saintliness, and the belief in a golden eternity. Gerard's death also had the effect of driving mother and father apart, and mother and son together. There were more arguments now. Leo tried to ease his gloom in drinking and gambling. Gabrielle took refuge in illnesses and the church. She went every day to light candles as well as to mass and confession, and criticized her husband for not being devout. Leo was a believer but said that he refused to support a corrupt institution. Jean-Louis, meanwhile, sought a richer world in his imagination, complete with Catholic terror as well as Gerard's angels. He was horrified, the day of Gerard's death, to see his uncles in the backyard setting off fireworks. Without really understanding, he felt the cruelty of the act.

Kerouac invented horse-racing games with marbles and baseball games with cards, kept elaborate statistics, and wrote and published little newspapers about the results. He also spent many hours in local theaters and movie houses where his father had free passes. This has been mentioned by all his biographers, but none have noted that because he didn't understand English, Jean-Louis had to imagine, in French, what was happening on stage or on the screen. His fantasies and his dreams were in French. In fact, Ti-Jean, as he was known after infancy, spoke not a word of English until he was six years old. He listened for hours to his uncle Mike's stories, told in joual, of the life of the family in Quebec. Most of his early schooling was in French. It wasn't until he was sixteen years old that he attended classes conducted entirely in English. He got good marks and even skipped grade six, but had to work hard, translating back and forth. Although he was a natural athlete and the best player on the football team, Kerouac was slow to grasp the plays, finding the jargon nearly incomprehensible.

After the death of his brother, and until high school, he was a lonely, withdrawn boy, his life encompassed by the French community of Lowell. Decades would pass before the French Canadians began to assimilate. As in Quebec, the Catholic Church dominated their lives.

Kerouac found the inhabitants mostly dull and ignorant, as he notes in *Doctor Sax*, and replaced them in his mind with characters such as Doctor Sax, who lived in a haunted gothic mansion high above the mills and the raging Merrimack River, having flown into town one midnight from Romania. And early in the book, he introduces La Poule Dupuin, a drunken priest and great storyteller.

Jack had heard that the big boys masturbated and thought he might give it a try one afternoon. He was alone in the house. His father was at the racetrack, his sister was outside playing, his mother and aunt had taken his dog Beauty for a walk. His mother and aunt let the dog run free and Beauty got run over by a car. Just as Jean-Louis was discovering his "tool" had "sensations in the tip," they yelled up to him, "Your dog is dead!"

Later, Kerouac commented, "They wonder why I'm mad."

Although Jack was moody and shy, by turns morose and manic, his specialness was obvious in high school. Girls fell all over him but he didn't know what to do about it. He forsook the beautiful, talented Peggy Coffey, already a singer with swing bands, for the plainer, presumably unattainable-unless-married Mary Carney. He'd later write one of his best books about this troubled high school romance.

He was, quite simply, smarter, better looking, and a better athlete than anybody else. He also had absolutely no ability or inclination to take advantage of these attributes. But his parents did; they wanted to channel his superiority into the immigrant's version of success which, in any language, translates into money. A good job — lawyer, maybe; big executive. But Jean-Louis already wanted to be a writer. To prepare for this goal, he haunted the public library, reading Goethe and, of all things, William Penn's *Maxims*. Believing it necessary to be acquainted with the full range of human knowledge, he read the entire *Encyclopaedia Britannica*. Because the other kids told him that writing was something only a "sissy" would want to pursue, he sought advice from the new young priest in town, Father Armand Morisette. The priest, known as Spike, remembered the boy, who was called Jean, saying, "Everybody is laughing at me."

Father Morisette thought the boy could be "a Napoleon or a movie star" — whatever he wished. The priest advised him to get out of town, go to New York.

He had been offered scholarships to play college football, and his father encouraged him to go to Boston College. But Jack chose Columbia University. Because he was a year younger than his classmates, Jack had to attend Horace Mann Prep School in Upper Manhattan. His classmates arrived at school in chauffeur-driven limousines; Jack got there after a two-and-a-half-hour subway ride from Brooklyn, where he was staying with his mother's stepsister. His wealthy fellow students took pity on him and his tawdry clothes, his butter sandwiches, his small-town ways. He was, after all, the star of the football team. His best friends were Eddie Gilbert, who later became a financial wizard, and Seymour Wyse, who introduced him to modern jazz.

The schoolwork at Horace Mann was no trouble; he did it on the long subway rides. But Jack took one look at downtown Manhattan and that was it. He managed to go to classes the first day, but the next he played hooky to wander the city, digging the characters, going to movies, reading at the public library.

He reported on Horace Mann sports activities for the *World-Telegram*, wrote a jazz column for the *Horace Mann Record*, published short stories in the literary magazine, and lost his virginity with a redheaded hooker in a Times Square hotel. Ninety percent of the students at Horace Mann were Jewish. Kerouac had never met a Jewish person, only heard about them in his father's rants, which he now could not comprehend. Also, for the first time, Jack encountered black people and was fascinated. When he brought Mary Carney to New York for the Horace Mann prom, she hated the city and everything that went with it, and Jack realized how his life had changed irrevocably.

Jack didn't attend graduation ceremonies that May of 1939 because he couldn't afford the white suit. He lay on the campus grass reading Whitman's *Leaves of Grass*.

Back in Lowell, he discovered the novels of Jack London and immediately decided he wanted to be a big adventurer too, documenting his life on the run. Also that summer, his friend Sebastian "Sammy" Sampas introduced him to the works of William Saroyan. Jack felt an immediate affinity with Saroyan's tender chronicles of small-town life, and decided to emulate him too. In fact, so taken were the boys with Saroyan's work, that Sammy wrote the famous author a letter expressing their admiration and bragging about his buddy Jack's own writing. The letter, to this day, is on display at the Saroyan Room of the Fresno City Museum.

It has been said that Kerouac's published works could be divided into the London writings (adventure) and the Saroyan works (Lowell novels), all of them infused with the spirit of Thomas Wolfe, whom he discovered the next semester at Columbia. But it was London's life, or the idea of it, and not the work, that influenced Kerouac. Critics have pointed to London's autobiographical *The Road* as a model for Kerouac's most famous work, but only the title is similar. The older book is a bleak, hard-bitten account of riding the rails. As for Kerouac's hometown novels — *Maggie Cassidy*, *Doctor Sax*, *Visions of Gerard* — they are driven by an imaginative power and religious mystery that sets them far beyond anything Saroyan achieved.

That summer, pressured by his father, Kerouac went to Boston College for a football tryout. The coach reported that Jack was the best halfback he had ever seen, but Kerouac still insisted on the big city, and that meant Columbia. There, besides studies and four hours a day of football, he washed dishes to pay for his meals. In the second game of the season, Jack broke his leg after a ninety-yard punt return. It might be called the Fatal Break, because despite a later, half-hearted attempt at football, and to recover his dream — inspired by old Bing Crosby movies — of being a clean-cut campus hero, Jack never went back to anything resembling a respectable life.

He smoked a pipe and read Thomas Wolfe, his leg in a cast propped up by the fireplace in the Lion's Den, and roamed New York on crutches.

Kerouac spent the next year wandering around, taking odd jobs, reading and writing. In the summer of 1942, he joined the merchant marine and shipped out of Boston for Greenland on the SS *Dorchester*. It was an eventful trip. The ship was twice attacked by torpedoes, Jack climbed a mountain in Greenland, and on the return voyage, he was arrested by the shore patrol in Sydney, Nova Scotia. He must have indeed felt like Jack London when the ship docked at Boston Harbor in October 1942. On its next voyage, the *Dorchester* was sunk by German U-boats and one thousand men were killed.

Kerouac returned to Columbia once more but couldn't take football or his studies seriously. Again, and for the last time, he quit school to seek more of the experience that he felt necessary for a writer. Jack moved into an apartment on 119th Street near the Columbia campus, with Edie Parker, who'd recently fled the upper-middle-class Detroit suburb of Grosse Pointe.

Jack enlisted in the navy and was called to report to boot camp in Newport, Rhode Island. The naval brass marked him for commando training, but Jack had no ability to take orders. One afternoon, he just put his rifle down on the drill field and walked to the library;

he was taken to the stockade and then the naval hospital. He was subjected to a battery of tests and it was discovered he had the highest IQ ever recorded in the history of the base. The assessment was "dementia praecox," which, when Jack was transferred to Bethesda Naval Hospital, was changed to "schizoid personality" with "angel tendencies." He was discharged as an "indifferent personality" in May 1943.

For several weeks, he divided his time between his parents' apartment in the Ozone Park section of Queens and Edie's place in Manhattan. In June 1943, Jack shipped out again, on the SS *George Weems*, which was taking bombs to Liverpool. The ship was attacked by German submarines on both legs of the trip. After docking in Liverpool, Jack took the train to London, went to a Tchaikovsky concert, and engaged the services of prostitutes.

He got back to New York in the fall, and began a season of meetings that by now have become a part of mythology. He moved in with Edie Parker at her new sixth-floor apartment on 118th Street. Her roommate was Joan Vollmer Adams. They listened to jazz, talked with Billie Holiday and Lester Young, became friends with Burl Ives and James T. Farrell. It was Edie who met Lucien Carr who one day brought seventeen-year-old Allen Ginsberg to the apartment. Ginsberg later said that he went with Lucien because he wanted to meet "the romantic seaman who wrote poem books." In talking with Kerouac, Ginsberg also realized that for the first time in his life he was being honest rather than posing as an intellectual. Ginsberg also fell in love with him.

Lucien was pale and frail, Jack dark and rugged, and both of them attracted plenty of attention from homosexuals. Occasionally, Kerouac would acquiesce to a come-on from a man, but always when drunk and never without later undergoing agonies of guilt. He never tried to hide these leanings; in fact, he openly discussed them, worried over them. As for women, he was passive, and practically, in the words of one girlfriend, LuAnne Henderson, "had to be raped." In this, as in everything else, Kerouac was completely open, admitting, most notably to Father Spike Morisette, that he thought of women as either whores or madonnas, and when he did have sex with women, he felt guilty for participating in the tragic cycle of birth and death. Perhaps when he was drunk and being promoted by a homosexual, Kerouac, in his blurry logic, excused his inclination precisely because he wouldn't be taking part in the cycle. He'd be guilty later.

Lucien was the obsession of a former teacher, David Kammerer, who had followed him from St. Louis to New York. It was Kammerer who introduced Jack and Edie to William Burroughs. Kammerer pursued Lucien, and news of him, like a vocation. One morning in August 1944, Lucien woke Jack and Edie, saying, "I got rid of the old man."

Kammerer, he claimed, had tried to rape him, and Lucien, in self-defense, stabbed the man and threw his body into the Hudson River. The story, repeated without any apparent skepticism by all biographers of the Beats, is that Lucien wanted Jack to help him dispose of the knife and Kammerer's glasses. But after killing a guy and tossing him in the river, Carr likely wouldn't have had any trouble getting rid of a knife and glasses. He could have dropped them through a sewer grate without Kerouac's help. Which is what he did anyway. It seems apparent that Lucien wanted company if he got busted. He had, after all, already called on Burroughs, who told him to go to the cops. But Jack was not the type to protect himself and he went along with his friend.

When Kerouac got back to 118th Street, the cops were waiting for him. He was held as a material witness to a homicide. His father wouldn't go his bail and called him a disgrace to the family. After Jack had spent a week in the Bronx jail, Edie's lawyer agreed to pay the money, but only when Edie and Jack were man and wife. A plainclothes cop, Police Detective John J. McKeon, escorted him to City Hall for the ceremony, signed the marriage certificate, and took the groom back to his cell. Jack spent his honeymoon night listening to the taunts of fellow prisoners.

Kerouac was released and Carr got two years in Elmira. Jack and Edie took the train to Michigan and a chauffeured limousine to the Parker family home in the wealthy suburb of Grosse Pointe. Edie's family owned steelyards, mills, and factories. "Your mother," Kerouac told her, "owns a shoe factory. My mother works in one."

He also told her that the Parker family mansion looked like a funeral home. Edie's sister Charlotte recalls that the only place Jack had any privacy was the bathroom, and he stayed in there for hours reading the Bible.

Using Parker family connections, Jack got a job as a night watchman at the Fruehof Corporation truck factory on the east side of Detroit. He worked the night shift, did his rounds as quickly as possible, and spent the rest of the time reading and writing. Evenings when he wasn't working, Jack made the local bars with Edie, their favorite being the Rustic Cabins Saloon, whose drinkers included no crazy poets or mad bopsters. There was no tragedy in Grosse Pointe either, as Kerouac emphasized in a letter that he left for Edie the day he returned to New York.

No sooner did he arrive than Kerouac met the Times Square junkie hustler and thief Herbert Huncke, who epitomized Jack's idea of "beat," being at the bottom of one's personality looking up, all the while incorporating the notion of beatific — blessed — or halfway to sainthood.

On May 1, 1945, the day New York papers carried the news of Hitler's death, Kerouac began writing his novel *The Town and the City*. He became friendly with a jazz piano player of Sicilian ancestry named Tom Livornese. The twenty-three-year-old Kerouac even escorted Tom's sixteen-year-old sister to her junior prom when her date, Ed White, another friend of Kerouac's, took sick. Maria remembers coming down the stairs that night at the family home in Lynbrook, New York, in her prom dress, Jack at the bottom with her father, both of them drinking Scotch: "He was lifting his glass to his mouth — and he just stopped. . . . He looked at me and said in French, 'How beautiful you are.'"

Later that summer, Jack and Maria, and Tom and his girlfriend, spent many nights at Jones Beach, swimming and looking up at the stars. Although Kerouac was shy, Maria was afraid: "I was in over my head."

Several years later, in 1953, they would start dating again. She'd visit him in Queens while his mother was at work, and Jack liked to take her to Times Square, to the bars, because "he liked to watch the winos drink their muscatel."

In the autumn of 1945, Kerouac almost died from thrombophlebitis. He stayed in the veteran's hospital and had death visions. He came out more serious about his writing and his religious beliefs. Then, in early 1946, his father died of stomach cancer. During Leo's last days, Kerouac nursed him in the Queens apartment, and started praying daily. After these two experiences, Kerouac no longer felt ashamed of expressing his affinity for Catholic mysticism in front of his intellectual friends.

There would soon be a new friend with whom he could certainly talk about religion as one former choirboy to another. This was a young man his Denver friends, Ed White and Al Hinkle, had been telling him about for a couple of years, a cowboy–pool hustler, jailbird–car thief, conman–womanizer nonpareil, a maniac of energy, and a just plain maniac. His name was Neal Cassady. When the two men met, each met his other half, and they handed each other the ticket to immortality.

Everyone who knew Neal thought he was the handsomest, most magnetic, most athletic man they'd ever met, and all Jack's friends thought the same thing about him. A party was arranged and, of course, the meeting turned out to be anti-climactic. They tiptoed around each other self-consciously, polite but slyly assessing. Neal had been lured away from Denver by the drop-dead gorgeous charms of one LuAnne Henderson. At that introductory party, LuAnne decided Jack was "prettier" than Neal, and made a play for him. But Jack never caught on. And right there was a big difference between Jack and Neal. Jack had to be practically hit over the head, and even after that happened, he never asked for anything. Neal needed only the hint of a hint to start operating, and he took everything anyone had to give.

Here's how Neal and LuAnne got to New York City: LuAnne won him from his other girlfriends and they took a bus to Sydney, Nebraska, to stay with her aunt and uncle. Neal worked in a gas station for a few days and LuAnne as a maid. After a week, they took off, LuAnne having stolen a few hundred bucks from her aunt and Neal having stolen the uncle's car. Vrrooom!

They left the car in a snowbank in Illinois and alighted from a Greyhound in Manhattan, Neal carrying a suitcase with jeans, T-shirts, and a copy of Marcel Proust's *Remembrance of Things Past*.

Once Kerouac and Cassady were able to go off together to talk, they became solid friends, and so began, for real, Kerouac's life on the road. Jack took off west in the summer of 1947, the trip that begins his most famous book, and for the next few years, with or without Neal Cassady, Kerouac collected the experiences that have now been elevated to the status of myth.

After every trip, Jack wound up back in Queens for a few months to write. He completed *The Town and the*

*City* in 1948, and immediately began two new novels, *Doctor Sax* and *On the Road*, this first version being a third-person account that featured Neal as "Walter Beauchamp" and himself as "Ray Smith." From the very beginning, no matter how many incarnations *On the Road* would go through, Kerouac conceived it as a religious parable, a holy search for meaning, a supercharged *Pilgrim's Progress*.

For the next several years, he'd alternate long periods of work at his mother's apartment, brief visits to the city for kicks, and cross-country trips to see Neal Cassady.

*The Town and the City* was sold to Harcourt Brace and published on March 2, 1950, and the first press notice of Jack Kerouac as a writer appeared in the *Denver Post* a few days later. It was by Justin Brierly, the Columbia alumnus who'd championed Ed White, Hal Chase, and Neal Cassady. Kerouac was soon making the rounds of literary events. At one party, as he related in a tape made fifteen years later for the Northport Long Island library, he met Carl Sandburg, who threw his arms around him, telling Jack, "You're just like me."

At the opera, he met Gore Vidal, who also wanted to throw his arms around Kerouac but didn't. At least not for a few more years. In his memoirs, Vidal would recall Kerouac's physical magnetism, the bead of water trickling down his forehead from "Indian black hair."

*The Town and the City* didn't sell. Kerouac took a series of short-lived jobs, began work on yet another book, *Visions of Cody*, and married Joan Haverty in November 1950. His writing style had begun to change after receiving letters from Neal Cassady that seemed to weave levels of time, experience, and memory into the same narrative line. He composed *Visions of Cody* like this and, wishing to capture the immediacy of the human voice, added transcriptions of conversations tape-recorded in Neal and Carolyn's living room.

Jack was living with Joan in an apartment at 454 W. Twentieth Street when he wrote the now legendary version of *On the Road* — in three weeks on Teletype paper. Actually, the manuscript consists of several twenty-foot-long sections of drawing paper scotch-taped together. This time Kerouac jettisoned literary experiments, forsook the influence of Wolfe and Melville for that of the Holy Ghost, letting it out in a mad rush, trusting in himself and the power of his spontaneous thoughts. He had the assistance of Benzedrine. At night, Jack set up a screen between his desk and the bed where his wife slept. He lost ten pounds during the period of composition and had to rewrite the last few feet of the manuscript because they were gobbled up by Lucien Carr's dog.

Editors and agents were not impressed by this work even after Kerouac had typed it, double-spaced, on letter-size white bond paper. One editor told him to stop wasting his considerable talents on insignificant characters.

He was at his mother's tiny Queens apartment, recovering from another serious attack of phlebitis and rewriting *On the Road* in French when he learned that Burroughs was in a Mexican prison for killing his wife Joan after she'd dared him to shoot a drink glass off her head.

He completed *Visions of Cody*, and rewrote *Doctor Sax* in two months at his sister's house in North Carolina, working at night by candlelight, writing in pencil. So there were two more books to add to his stack of unpublished material. Meanwhile, John Clellon Holmes' Beat novel, *Go*, was published by Scribner's, who'd rejected *On the Road*. Kerouac was in San Francisco working for the Southern Pacific as a yard clerk, living in the Cassady attic, and sharing Carolyn with Neal, experiences that later figured in an abominable motion picture, *Heart Beat*. He went to Mexico and returned to New York on the bus just as Holmes was banking a $20,000 check for the paperback rights to *Go*.

Kerouac's annoyance over Holmes' success was mollified somewhat when Holmes published his *New York Times Magazine* piece, "This Is the Beat Generation," in November 1953 and credited Kerouac with coining the term. Holmes called it a "spiritual movement."

Kerouac had been corresponding with an editor named Robert Lax who was a convert to Catholicism. When they finally met, the conversation was entirely on religious matters. When Kerouac expressed his desire to go on retreat, Lax offered to get him into a monastery in France, but by the time it was arranged, Jack's head had been turned by Buddhism. Although his studies were serious and deep, and his commitment to Buddhism lasted for years, it had a negative effect on his work. It certainly did on his life. In his writing, the Kerouac sound and distinct descriptive magic — the thing described and the heart of the thing described — were too often replaced by mere reference to Buddhist terminology. Later, even icy Bill Burroughs would chastise Kerouac for retreating into Buddhism and away from his native warmth and feeling.

It seems obvious that the further Kerouac got into Buddhism, the unhappier he became. But, of course, it was his vast unhappiness that had led him to Buddhism in the first place. His marriages and all his relations with women had failed, he'd gotten no reward from his writing, his family called him a bum, and he knew he was on his way to becoming a serious drunk. Catholicism appeared to have failed him and he was looking for a replacement, something to shield him from the bleak Nothingness. Jack Kerouac was desperate to believe that everything was a dream and he wasn't really suffering.

In Queens, Jack wrote *Maggie Cassidy*, the story of his teenage romance with Mary Carney in Lowell. Then he went to Mexico again, tried to get a job with the railroad in Montreal, did get on with the Southern Pacific in San Luis Obispo, lasted a month, shipped out as a waiter in the officers' mess on the SS *William Carruth*, and signed off in New Orleans. Back in New York, he had the affair with the black subterranean woman he called Mardou Fox, and when it was over went home to his mother's apartment and wrote a book about it in three Benzedrine days.

The next couple of years held more traveling, more books completed, and more disappointment. Given how unhappy he was at times, it is a testament to his openness and generosity that Kerouac was able to keep making new friends, many of whom remained close until the end of his life. In Mexico, he fell in with an old-time junkie called Bill Garver and an Indian girl, Esperanza Villanueva, whom he'd later write about as Tristessa. In California, he was brought into an entirely new circle that included Kenneth Rexroth, Gary Snyder, Robert Creeley, John Montgomery, Robert Duncan, Philip Lamantia, and Philip Whalen.

Back at his sister's house in North Carolina in 1955, he wrote *Visions of Gerard* at Christmastime. He had completed seven major books in two years, all unpublished.

The next summer, Kerouac worked as a forest-fire lookout on Desolation Peak in Washington State near the British Columbia border. His two months there cured him of the illusion he could ever be a true hermit. He came down from the mountain and arrived in San Francisco in the midst of a cultural renaissance. *Howl* had been accepted by Lawrence Ferlinghetti's City Lights press and *On the Road* had finally found a home, with Viking Press.

Journals and reviews asked for work by Jack and Allen. The two writers went into bars and coffee shops to find their reputations had preceded them.

The emergence of Kerouac and Ginsberg, and later Burroughs, Corso, Snyder, and the rest, coincided with a general upheaval in American cultural life, for Elvis Presley had already begun to revolutionize America.

Say what one may about the Fifties, North American values had never, and have never since, experienced a knockout combination such as that delivered by Presley and Kerouac. They exploded onto the mainstream media scene within months of each other. Kerouac's first appearance in *Time*, that barometer, was in September 1957, just three months after the magazine discovered Elvis. In *Time*'s review, the protagonist of *On the Road*, Dean Moriarty, "swaggering" in his "amorality," was compared to Petronius Arbiter's "rascally Encolpius, who lived by his wits in Nero's fat and frightened time." They had described Elvis much the same way.

Both Kerouac and Presley were good-looking, disenfranchised, and unlike anything else that had gone before. Imagine the young man or young woman bored with the Four Lads on the radio, bored with the latest novel by James Gould Cozzens (*Time* cover person the week before *On the Road* was reviewed), never knowing there's something else out there, or believing somehow that there must be — *has* to be. And he or she spins the dial on the plastic portable radio and hears, "Ready, set, go man go!" or opens up *On the Road* and reads, "Go, go, go!" — and he or she is gone.

Or they just see their pictures, see them on the Steve Allen show. Elvis first, Jack a few months later. Jack looking like Elvis' older, tougher, half-brother. Both raw and dangerous, their stances hinting at mysterious delights that may have something to do with negritude and definitely have something to do with sex. Imagine if you were that young woman's or that young man's parent.

Of course, both men were deeply religious and too attached to their mothers.

Back in New York, Jack began a love affair with a woman named Helen Weaver. He and Allen were hailed on the street by strangers. Jack and Allen met Salvador Dali at the Russian Tea Room, and Dali interrupted Allen's enthusing over Marlon Brando, pointed at Jack, and declared, "He is more beautiful than Brando."

When Jack's drinking got out of hand and he proved unreliable, Helen threw him out. He moved into the Marlton Hotel and soon met Joyce Glassman. In February, he sailed to Tangiers on a Yugoslavian freighter and was reunited with William Burroughs. He helped type a manuscript Burroughs was working on and gave the text a name, *Naked Lunch*.

Soon tired of Morocco, Kerouac traveled through France to Paris and on to London and finally home, where from a Tangiers rooftop he had dreamed of eating Wheaties in the morning in Florida. But no sooner was Jack back than he went on the road with his mother, traveling to Berkeley, where they set up housekeeping in a cottage rented with his advance money from Viking.

Kerouac was already notorious. Malcolm Cowley, on the last page of his book *The Literary Situation*, prophesied that Jack Kerouac was the American writer of the future. Jack was interviewed by a reporter from the *San Francisco Examiner*. When Joyce Glassman called him at The Place, a jazz hangout in San Francisco, the bartender said, "Kerouac? Everybody wants to talk to him."

His mother was dissatisfied with California, so Kerouac, with two months to go before the publication of *On the Road*, took her back to Florida, and almost immediately left for Mexico City. He arrived back in Orlando on the first of September, 1957, and two days later, got on that Greyhound for New York.

# FOUR

"Yet I lusted to thieve, and did it. . . . What then did wretched I so love in thee, thou theft of mine, thou deed of darkness, in that sixteenth year of my age?"

— St. Augustine

"Hold it, fellas. That don't move me. Let's get real, real gone for a change."

— Elvis Presley

No one to whom Jack Kerouac's writing matters can avoid getting personal about the impact of *On the Road*, and the lasting significance of his other works. *On the Road* may not be his best book, but it is the one that jolted most people's sensibilities and changed their lives.

Me, I was a month from my seventeenth birthday, it was June 1962, and I was no angel. I'd just been freed from custody after being wrongfully charged in an episode involving a car, another guy, his knife, and his girlfriend. Although my innocence was eventually established, it was obvious even to me that the path I was on led to more trouble and more after that. I would probably have some fun along the way, but

I could already see the shadow of the Big House.

Friday night I stepped out of the Black Maria and the next morning claimed my old job back at a place in Clifton Heights, Pennsylvania, called the Bazaar of All Nations. It was a vast cinderblock building, the inside given over to shops and stalls; it didn't resemble a shopping mall but rather a market such as I would later see in Africa and Central America. I worked at a place that sold caramel popcorn, and on Saturdays had to put in a thirteen-hour shift. I mixed the ingredients, prepared the concoction in large motorized copper pots, and sold it in various-sized bags. During busy periods it was dumb work; at other times it was dumb and boring. It was dumb and boring that Saturday — so boring, in fact, that I closed up for fifteen minutes at lunch time, one o'clock, to wander around the Bazaar. I looked at the ladies in the jury-rigged beauty shop, heads stuck up into the huge egg-cup driers, browsed through records (and can still in my mind see one album cover I studied that Saturday afternoon — Santo and Johnny), and finally, right before heading back to the caramel corn, with only a few minutes to spare, I went into the bookstore. Store — it was actually, like most of the operations, delineated from the other vendors by curtains and scrap-wood partitions. The paperbacks were all in cardboard boxes, each section designated by a cardboard sign on which was written: LLAAFFs, SSSEX! or Sports. I went to Sports to buy something — being a nice kid, if a rowdy one — for my nine-year-old brother. I got him a biography of Babe Ruth. Then I grabbed two from SSSEX! One was about a good-looking young kid's rise

# The Long Slow Death of Jack Kerouac 35

to the top of the pop-music business, back-cover copy indicating all the girls perched on the rungs of the ladder of his success with skirts hiked up to there. The other was about characters careening across country in automobiles in search of kicks. I got my three for a quarter and hustled back to the caramel corn.

Hardly anyone was interested in caramel corn that day. In fact, there were few people in the Bazaar. It was, or so I'd been told, sunny outside. With nothing to do, I sat on burlap sacks of demerara sugar in the back room, door open, one eye on the counter, and started on the paperback about the would-be teen idol. I gave up after a few pages. The kid was a creep, his music was of even less interest than the guitar stylings of Santo and Johnny, and the sex scenes were dull. I had no interest in the mighty Babe. The back cover of the third book had a tiny photo of the author in the bottom left corner. He was a rugged-looking guy who needed a shave. It said that he'd been in the merchant marine and roamed around aplenty.

I started reading. I was hooked from the first line. And that first line, the first page, even the way the page looked, has remained burned in mind, just as the characters burned like roman candles. "I first met Dean not long after . . ."

Immediately, I began to live with the characters in *On the Road*. I didn't read the book so much as I experienced it. Probably for the first time since childhood games, I was so thoroughly absorbed that I had no thought of myself or for myself. The odd time a customer called, I filled the order as if in a trance.

Dean Moriarty answering the door wearing only his

shorts, reminding the author of a young Gene Autry, and nodding his head, "Yes, . . . yes," like a boxer getting instructions . . . Sal Paradise waking up in a midwestern hotel room not knowing where he was or who he was . . . the Mexican girl on the low-down streets of South L.A. . . . the ride in the hay truck with hoboes and tramps . . . tank empty, coasting downhill with the clutch in, siphoning gas while the attendant slept . . . bashing out rhythms on the dashboard while Symphony Sid spun wild radio bop . . . the ghost of the Susquehanna walking in circles around Harrisburg . . . sleeping on top of the car in the Mexican jungle after a wild mambo night in a whorehouse . . . George Shearing as God . . . God as Pooh Bear . . . Dean's father, the Larimer Street bum they never found.

Of course, I had not a clue that the book was already famous and those scenes which to me were fraught with such import — for reasons I didn't quite understand and couldn't explain — had already meant much the same to others, and would keep on doing so. I didn't know I was collaborating in a myth.

I've spoken to people who, upon reading *On the Road*, immediately quit their jobs, their schools, and set out for adventure. Often they put aside an entire way of thinking about the world, and their own world widened with new music to listen to, new books to read — but the most important, and most overlooked, of the gifts in that book, and all others written by Kerouac, is the gift of compassion.

I had already been on the road and was acquainted with jazz music, but I didn't know anyone else with similar experiences or like interests. At age twelve, I'd

## The Long Slow Death of Jack Kerouac 37

begun running away from home. We'd moved from the city to the suburbs, and I didn't like it. That first trip I was away six weeks, hiking, hitchhiking, even climbing on a freight train a time or two. In my part of the country, one didn't see much of this sort of thing, and I never met anyone near to my age who was on the bum. When I was fourteen, after four such trips, I realized I'd best finish school before taking off for good. On one adventure, I'd traveled with an old Russian tramp, a White Russian who claimed to be a count, and I had no reason to doubt him. He professed to be shocked when I admitted that I didn't read books and his parting words to me — on a highway near Schenectady, New York — were to extract a promise that I would begin to read. I did read too, but not what he had in mind, mainly books about fixing cars or stories about kids who fixed cars. *On the Road* was the first book that the Count would have sanctioned.

Not only did I fix cars, but shortly after I stopped running away from home I began to steal them. Not for larcenous reasons, not to vandalize them, and not for the hell of it. I just loved cars, and couldn't wait two years to get my own driver's license. I'd take them from parking lots, drive around, and return them later to another section of the same lot. I stole dozens. Unlike Neal Cassady, I didn't get caught. Like him, I was always on the lookout for willing girls, but unlike him, I didn't find many. In my town, I was the guy least likely to have a date. I was neither a brain, an athlete, a greaser, a straight-arrow, nor what was called a fairy. I was closest to a hoodlum, but there was just a little something that wasn't quite right. These distinctions were exactly defined and cruel, and if you didn't precisely fit one or the other, you had to damn well make the proper adjustments if you wished to get along. And I also knew about jazz which, when I mentioned it to my schoolmates, elicited blank stares or hostility. It may be difficult to imagine now, but in those days there was, or was supposed to be, a definite communist menace. It often came disguised as a jazz musician.

On my fifteenth birthday, my older cousin Bill, who lived in Virginia, and could play trumpet and drums, gave me three record albums: Dave Brubeck's *Take Five*, a Verve jazz sampler, and an LP of bongo music. He must have sensed something about me.

I already listened to stations that played all black music by which I do not mean Motown — which was known by many blacks as Oreo music — but, rather, hard bop, and real R&B. I also tuned in to WWVA out of Wheeling, West Virginia, to hear genuine country music.

The point of all this is to note that, unlike a lot of people with whom I later spoke about these matters, I was prepared for *On the Road*. The experiences therein related were not entirely alien to me. True, I was anxious to have more of the same. To roar down that road in a car, any car. To find girls and great buddies, to dig those wild sounds in person, and I now wanted to read books. Kerouac supplied a reading list. One week books meant nothing to me and the next I was checking Eugene Sue's *Mysteries of Paris* out of the library because Dean Moriarty gave it to Sal Paradise to read on his bus trip from San Francisco to New York.

Just the other day, I held in my hands, thanks to my

## The Long Slow Death of Jack Kerouac 39

friend Rod Anstee, the very same book, the actual copy of *Mysteries of Paris*, that Neal gave to Jack. It had a library binding, pages the color of nicotine stains, and it seemed appropriate that Neal had stolen it from the San Francisco Public Library. (The book is very much like a holy relic — the tibia, for instance, of St. Theresa, Jack Kerouac's favorite saint.)

So my life turned in a new direction, though not only because I discovered travel and worthwhile music, and began to read, but because I learned that my interests and enthusiasms were not pathological as I'd been led to believe — that, in fact, they were inclinations worthy of celebration in a book, a book that was not merely anecdotal, a book I must have realized intuitively was important literature.

I went to the library for other books but apart from the 600 section where they keep the motor manuals, it was terra incognita. I didn't know how to navigate, but I did come across something called *World Authors*, a great thick reference book with writers' biographies and often pictures. I looked for people who'd knocked around, had adventures. My method was hit-or-miss, to be sure, but I don't think I wasted time reading bad books; on the other hand, my naïveté lead me to people like Joseph Conrad and Herman Melville.

I discovered there was a literary tradition of rough hustling, of celebrating the open road. In America alone there had been Walt Whitman and Mark Twain, Jack London and Jim Tully, Henry Miller and John Dos Passos, as well as an entire hobo literature and dozens of hobo books. Later, I wondered why it was that Kerouac's book transcended the others.

Not too long after reading *On the Road*, I discovered the works of Robert Lowry, particulary *The Big Cage*, in which his autobiographical hero covers much the same territory during the same years as Kerouac's characters. Kerouac's friend John Clellon Holmes not only recorded similar experiences, he used characters he'd been introduced to by Kerouac and even employed titles that Kerouac gave him, such as *Go* and *The Horn*.

Why weren't the lives of millions of people throughout the world changed by reading Robert Lowry and John Clellon Holmes? It is not merely because Kerouac is a superior writer. He was primarily a religious writer. Not an explicator or apologist for Christianity, nor an obvious didact like Thomas Merton, but, far more powerfully, a writer whose message is one of compassion, and almost the entire body of his work is suffused with religious mysticism. The writer he most resembles is not Thomas Wolfe, or James Joyce, or any of the others he's been compared to, but the Bishop of Hippo himself, St. Augustine. In fact, entire passages from each man's confessions are interchangeable.

Of course, I didn't realize all this until much later. But what I did respond to from the beginning was enough: the writer's great heart was as wide open as the road itself.

# FIVE

"Look, you're young. I'm twenty-six, I've got to fuck him now before it's too late."
— Woman (a stranger) to Joyce Glassman

Jack and Joyce were awakened in the morning by a telephone call from Keith Jennison, one of Kerouac's editors at Viking, who offered congratulations and announced he was coming right over with a case of champagne. While they were waiting, Kerouac related the dream he'd had that night in which he was being followed by a gang of children chanting his name. He had a head wound wrapped with a bandage, and was on the run, leading his army of followers into Mongolia. But suddenly there he was in the Victory Theatre, having narrowly eluded the Fame Police.

But it was only a dream. In real life there would be no victory. Jennison arrived and so did the media. From the very beginning, reporters wanted to harp on the nihilism and violence they purported to find in the Beat Generation. Joyce remembers Jack's patience and courtesy with them, saying, " 'Beat means beatific, see?' "

In order to deal with them, Kerouac downed the champagne, bottle after bottle. As Jennison was leaving, he took Joyce aside and shook his head sadly.

"Take care of this man," he pleaded.

She tried to, warned Jack that he mustn't assume interviewers were his friends. But Jack was too honest. He "failed to protect that deep visionary part of himself."

At WOR-TV in New York, John Wingate, host of *Nightbeat*, asked him what he was looking for. "I'm waiting for God to show me His face," Jack replied.

He had spoken the truth, but it didn't resemble anything anyone wanted to hear.

He was sucked into a vortex of parties, and interviews, openings, readings, and brawls. The first review of *On the Road* was the last good review, and bad reviews followed him to the grave, and still weren't content. No serious writer has ever been so vilified.

Jack, who had kept a scrapbook of clippings attesting to his athletic achievements, must have been horrified to check his new notices against his old.

"The visiting squad formed a vague background for the brilliant running of Kerouac," proclaimed the *New York Herald Tribune* in 1939.

"Kerouac writes like a slob running a temperature," proclaimed the *Hudson Review* in 1957.

And knowing that Kerouac became close friends and drinking buddies with Jackson Pollock, one can just imagine them in their cups. They were both notorious for overhauling their art — Kerouac with spontaneous prose, Pollock with abstract impressionism — and both paid the price. Imagine them bemoaning their reviews. "Did you hear Truman Capote's quip about me?" Jack asking Pollock. " 'That's not writing, that's typing.' " — Pollock replying, "Yeah, Kerouac, but they looked at my work and said, 'A chimpanzee could do it.'"

When *The Subterraneans* was published in 1958, *Time* called Kerouac "the latrine laureate of bohemia." There would be far worse, but nothing hurt him so much as the cruelty displayed by a former friend, Kenneth Rexroth. Originally from the Midwest, Rexroth came to California in the Twenties and, by the Fifties, considered the Bay Area arts world his own little fiefdom. A polymath and mythomaniac, Rexroth assumed the role of knower of all and doer of everything. After submitting his autobiography, Rexroth's editor reportedly commented, "Kenneth, you don't really expect anyone's going to believe this shit."

The book was finally published as *An Autobiographical Novel*. True or not, it is classic Americana. The man was also a translator, critic, and composer of the some of the greatest love poems of the modern era. But, as well, Kenneth Rexroth demanded his superiority be acknowledged. He was jealous, envious, spiteful, and malicious.

Before he met the author, and before *On the Road* was published, Rexroth praised Kerouac's writing in print. But once Jack's work began to appear, Rexroth acted like Kerouac was a usurper of his terrain. He pursued a vicious little sideline of demeaning Jack Kerouac, who had no defenses of any sort, much less against ferocious former friends. "*The Subterraneans* is about jazz and Negroes," Rexroth wrote in *The Nation*. "Now if there is anything Jack knows nothing about, it's jazz and Negroes."

Now, I don't know how much Kenneth Rexroth knew about blacks, but I've heard the records he made reading poetry to jazz, and I do know the man didn't have any rhythm. He's also the fellow who wrote that there's nothing in Charlie Parker that's not in Beethoven.

Rexroth has a minor role in *The Subterraneans* where Kerouac slyly calls him Rheinhold Cacoethes. Someone has pointed out that "cacoethes" in German denotes a mania for scribbling. But Kerouac knew from drinking beer in Mexico that "cacahuetes" in Spanish means peanuts.

Kerouac's drinking increased, although those who knew him might have thought such a thing impossible. Pulled this way and that, he tried to go along with everyone. Women would offer themselves, and he'd take them, whether Joyce was there or not. Men wanted to beat up Jack because their girlfriends were after him. Jack, who abhorred violence and wouldn't fight back, suffered the beatings.

One night in the Village, a man attacked Kerouac outside a bar, knocked him to the ground and began pounding his head against the curb. After the attacker was chased off, a jazz piano player named Graham Cournoyer heard Kerouac muttering in French and came to his aid. Cournoyer, from Montreal, answered him in French, and thus began a friendship. Not only did the two men have music and language in common, Cournoyer was from the Old Country, a guy Jack could take home and introduce to his mother.

Joyce finally gave up on him, and Jack started going out wth Gary Snyder's sister Thea. But she couldn't take it for long, later saying she'd never seen anyone drink so much or smoke so much pot, or act so unpredictably. One minute, he'd say his big dream was to go live in the woods with Gary, and the next moment he was going to head to Hollywood and pal around with his idol Frank Sinatra.

That winter in New York, he read poetry backed by a trio led by composer and French-horn player David Amram. Cournoyer was a friend of Amram's and often played piano on these gigs. Later, Jack was booked into the Village Vanguard, a gig that was a fiasco from the beginning. Kerouac, on stage in sport jacket and tie, reading spontaneous bop prosody to an uncomprehending audience. They booed, and as the nights went on there were fewer to boo. John Montgomery, who'd been hiking in Vermont, came into the Vanguard one evening with his rucksack and the staff gave him dirty looks. Kerouac later told Montgomery the engagement was cut short because management complained about too many bums showing up with rucksacks. The date was rescued, one night anyway, by the versatile Steve Allen who, picking up on the musical quality of Kerouac's voice, came out of the audience to back him on the piano. The result was so impressive that Dot Records signed them to do an album.

Kerouac escaped madness by taking refuge, literally, in the church. He began attending mass and reading St. John of the Cross, universally regarded as one of the greatest mystical writers.

Early in 1958, Kerouac bought a house in Northport, New York, on Long Island. Jerry Wald of Twentieth Century Fox offered $100,000 for the film rights to *On the Road*, with the stipulation that Dean Moriarty be killed at the end in a fiery car crash like that other Dean, James. Kerouac refused.

The rights were eventually sold to Tri-Way Productions, and Kerouac received $2,500 as an advance. The company cast the picture with Cliff Robertson as Sal Paradise, Mort Sahl as Dean Moriarty, and folded — gratefully — before the project could go any farther.

Kerouac could hide in church or hide in Northport, but not for long. Gangs of people would show up looking for the famous author. He might go to the liquor store and not come back for two weeks. One night he got into a cab in the Village with his new girlfriend, Dodie Müller, former wife of the painter Jan Müller, and when a mob of women recognized Kerouac, they started rocking the cab, eventually pulling him out. He was on his back in the street and they had stripped off most of his clothes before Müller and the cab driver were able to come to his rescue.

Graham Cournoyer recalls walking into bars with Jack around this time: "We'd go into a place like the Cedars and there'd be, say, thirty women in there. Maybe six knockouts, and Jack could have anyone of them. It was hot like that for a long time. A long enough time to kill anyone. And Jack would do it, but he also drank like a motherfucker. And to get a hard-on, well ... Look, there was a Village poet, Brigitte Mernaghan, who absolutely worshipped Jack's body. She was real Irish, tall, crazy. She told me she had Jack in the sack at least a hundred times. Sucking his cock, worshipping him. And all that time never once did he come."

Jack befriended the photographer Robert Frank and wrote the preface for his book of photographs, *The*

## The Long Slow Death of Jack Kerouac  47

*Americans*. Kerouac also collaborated with Frank and his partner, Alfred Leslie, on a film made from the third act of an unpublished, unproduced play Kerouac wrote at the suggestion of Lillian Hellman. The film, shot in black and white, is called *Pull My Daisy*, after a nonsense ditty Kerouac had composed years earlier with Allen Ginsberg. The characters, including Ginsberg, Amram, Corso, and the painter Larry Rivers, are silent during the film, but Kerouac provided narration which was subsequently praised by film — if not literary — critics. The narration was dubbed, Kerouac having been banned from the set, a loft in Greenwich Village, for introducing real bums and winos to the proceedings.

During the production of the film, Jack became friendly with Walter Gutman, who published a Wall Street market report, and raised the money for *Pull My Daisy*. When the idea of the film was presented to him, Gutman began to read books once more, starting with *On the Road*. He sent a note, telling Kerouac "the book opened up again for me what writing could be." It was Gutman who picked the name of the film.

They first met at the Hansa Gallery in New York, during a retrospective show of paintings by Jan Müller. Gutman saw Kerouac sitting in the gallery, sober, neat, and clean, and somehow like he didn't belong. "He was a photogenic, handsome man — with markably luminous eyes — but still there was something about the contour of his cheeks, his haircut, the shirt he wore . . . that made me think that, famous or not, he looked like a bum."

As Gutman came to know Kerouac better, he admired him more. "His life was built not only on talent but on physical strength and daring." Gutman was astounded that Kerouac was nonviolent, for he moved like a fighter and had the "face of a real battler."

One Halloween weekend, Gutman was on Long Island with a girlfriend, a black dancer. He had been seeing the woman off and on for a few years and although they got along physically, there wasn't much conversation. Not knowing what to do on a Saturday morning, they drove in Gutman's Porsche to Kerouac's home in Northport.

I find it interesting, Gutman's report of Mémère — as Kerouac's mother was known — answering the door and welcoming the couple. Although Jack was just waking up, "his mother insisted we come in." Now here is a Jewish man showing up at the door with a black woman, and Mémère, who is always presented in biographies as a racist ogre, "insists" they come in. She was always hospitable to Stanley Twardowicz, a Pole; Vic Gioscia, a Sicilian; Robert Boles, a black; and so many others. Mémère was particularly fond of unabashed hell-raisers like Graham Cournoyer and, later, Cliff Anderson.

How can this be explained? There is no mystery. I believe it is simply because these people displayed a native, bread-and-butter courtesy and respect, and didn't come in with an agenda or come on like "beatniks" or "hippies."

So Gutman, his friend, and Jack spent the entire morning and afternoon in Kerouac's room, talking. Gutman was impressed that Jack and the woman could communicate freely. "This was the happiest time I had with Jack . . . when he was sober he was brilliantly and sensitively aware of you. . . . "

Kerouac wrote *The Dharma Bums* in three weeks in November of 1958, and when the book appeared it was an instant success with readers, even though the author was parodied on national television by comedian Louis Nye as "Jack Crackerjack," shouting hysterically, "Kill for the sake of killing!"

Cournoyer recalls that in 1959, after *The Dharma Bums* had been published, Jack called him with news that he'd gotten them work on the railroad. At first, Cournoyer didn't believe he was serious, "but Jack would do crazy things like that. He also probably wanted to get away from being 'Jack Kerouac.'"

The job was pulling spikes on the tracks near East Orange, New Jersey. "We worked ten to four," says Cournoyer. "But it wasn't long before we started drinking on the job. After four days, Jack walked away from the gig and I followed. The Italian foreman ran after us to fire us. But the really strange thing is that a couple days later Jack got us the job back, telling the guy this incredible story about somebody in the family dying. We worked another entire week and had a ball. Pulling spikes, bullshitting, and drinking."

Kerouac had been invited to appear on Steve Allen's TV show but was so nervous he couldn't get on the train, and at the last minute, had to catch a plane. On November 16, 1959, with Steve noodling in the background, Kerouac gave a remarkable performance, his voice melodic and resonant.

Back at Northport, Jack had to build a high fence around his property and another fence around his patio, yet the fans still got in, one waking him at five in the morning, leaning over the bed, "You busy?"

He must have wondered whether this sort of thing happened to his contemporaries — John Updike, for instance, who, in the *New Yorker*, had portrayed Jack and Neal on tricycles, making like Dharma Bums in the neighborhood till their mothers called them in to dinner.

Those long nights in his study, spinning the radio dial searching for jazz, he didn't come across anyone doing a tune called "Updikey," but there was one called "Kerouazy," by a guy named Don Morrow, backed by Doc Severinson on trumpet. It was on an album called *Grimm's Hip Fairy Tales*. The song wasn't much, but at least it wasn't as ridiculous as "Beatnik Fly" by Jay and the Hurricanes or Paul Revere and the Raiders' "Beatnik Sticks."

Those long nights in his study, listening to jazz, Kerouac had begun to have intense religious visions. Staring at a picture of Cardinal Giovanni Montini, he envisioned him as pope and painted him in papal robes. Four years later Montini became Pope Paul VI. When a reporter came to call, he noted the crucifix over the bed and Kerouac told him he kissed it every night, "the silent kiss," before going to bed.

This is the man in whose name appeared exploitation films such as *The Beatniks*, the poster for which features a drawing of a leather-jacketed hoodlum holding a knife to the throat of a girl whose breasts are about to escape her ripped blouse; a background photo shows beatniks robbing a store.

*High School Confidential* had the Feds infiltrating a high school to catch beatnik drug pushers. Phillipa Fallon played a teenaged Beat poetess, and recited a poem, "High School Drag," later released as a 45 on MGM, with the line, "Turn your eyes inside/And dig the vacuum."

Roger Corman directed *A Bucket of Blood*, about a beatnik busboy-sculptor who kills people then covers them with clay. And in *Visit to a Small Planet*, an alien, Jerry Lewis, meets a Beat chick. Beatnik Shirley MacLaine bops Robert Mitchum in *Two for the Seesaw*; Carolyn Jones is a beatnik party girl in Frank Capra's *A Hole in the Head*. There were English beat movies and even a Canadian one, *The Bloody Brood*, which gave Peter Falk his first major role — as a killer Beat.

Albert Zugsmith, who was responsible for *High School Confidential*, made another trip to the well with Jackie Coogan and Mamie Van Doren, producing *The Beat Generation*. (He had registered the title.) This one was about a beatnik rapist who held court at a Venice Beach coffee shop where there was a lot of far-out action, including poetry readings by Vampira, the TV horror-movie hostess who appeared in Ed Wood films such as *Plan Nine from Outer Space*. The movie was popular enough, evidently, to inspire a television offshoot that featured beatniks terrorizing shop owners. Kerouac wrote a letter to *Escapade* magazine, publisher of his monthly "Last Word" column: "I am completely amazed by this insulting ugliness about kids who read books and read poems in coffee shops." (Two letters published above Kerouac's column take him to task for a recent piece on bullfighting in which he displayed sympathy for the bull. One correspondent refers to "neurotics and cowards who follow his [Kerouac's] philosophy and works.")

The only movie that pretended to seriousness was one of the worst; this was *The Subterraneans*, and it purportedly had something to do with Kerouac's book of the same name. The Kerouac character was played by George Peppard, and the black woman, Mardou Fox, by a white woman, Leslie Caron. But, at least, it had some good music by Gerry Mulligan.

In the midst of all this, Kerouac prayed and read and drank. His new friend Vic Gioscia, a jazz piano player and sociology professor at the Catholic Fordham University, reported they'd sit in Jack's room listening to jazz and discussing St. John of the Cross. Gioscia arranged for Kerouac to go on the Fordham radio show *Dialogue* to discuss religion. Kerouac said on air that religious distinctions shouldn't really matter if you were able to attain another spiritual dimension. Hearing this, Cardinal Spellman notified the station that such talk was henceforth forbidden on Fordham radio.

So Kerouac was getting it from everywhere. He decided to escape by accepting Lawrence Ferlinghetti's invitation to hide out in his Bixby Canyon cabin at Big Sur on the Pacific Coast south of Monterrey. Jack would live like Henry David Thoreau with an occasional visit from Ferlinghetti for the purpose of going through Kerouac's collection of dream sketches. It was a pretty idea, and Jack was no doubt sincere as he boarded the train at Grand Central Station. But when did his resolve vanish? I see him in his cabinette staring out at the night in Illinois, pulling on his bottle of Scotch, seeing the sad-eyed puffy face that had replaced the handsome one in the reflection in the window. Illinois!

He probably came to what passed for his senses somewhere around Harrisburg, where years before he'd seen the ghost of the Susquehanna. Anyway, he hit San Francisco after a few days and headed up to North Beach, bursting through the doors of the City Lights Bookstore — the King of the Beats on a Saturday night.

Kerouac did make it to Bixby Canyon, but not until he had gone on a drunken rampage, made new friends, lost old ones, gotten engaged — according to the gossip columns — been thrown out of bars, grocery stores, restaurants, and private homes, and seen death everywhere. One night's spree was particularly unfortunate because he missed his appointment with Henry Miller, who was the only major writer to have taken him seriously, or, at least, the only major writer with the courage to praise him in print. Miller had written the preface to *The Subterraneans*, asking, "Where does he get that stuff? From you and me, from staying up all night . . ."

At Ferlinghetti's cabin, Jack suffered a nervous breakdown, but eventually managed to drag himself across country and home to Northport.

Throughout his life, Kerouac staggered between extremes of behavior and, as he got closer to the end, the extremes became more violent. He was such a drunk — and in the matter of literary drinkers, he had no competition, not Malcolm Lowry or Brendan Behan, or any of them — he was such a drunk that you have to wonder at the reserves of physical and mental strength he was able to summon forth. Back on Long Island, he was able to sit down and write *Big Sur* in ten days.

This death-haunted drunken chronicle has been compared unfavorably — and unjustly, I think — to Malcolm Lowry's *Under the Volcano*. But Lowry's book is so overwritten that the reader is held at a safe distance. It's not scary. Kerouac is not interested in making a well-crafted novel — he wants to confess and to convey his horror. And he succeeds. It might be said, however, that *Under the Volcano* is more a drunkard's book, if only because of its solipsism. Lowry's writing calls to mind a lush, albeit an eloquent if overprecious one, emoting on and on through the night, thrilled at hearing his own voice, unmindful of whether or not anyone gives a shit.

After completing *Big Sur*, Kerouac treated himself to a case of cognac and woke two weeks later in a hospital with no memory of how he got there.

Earlier, in January 1961, along with Allen Ginsberg, and under the direction of Timothy Leary, Kerouac had his first experience with psilocybin. Later that year he took LSD with the same pair, and Leary recorded him saying, "Walking on water wasn't built in a day."

In the fall, he went with his mother to Orlando to visit his sister and her husband who were living in a house Jack had bought with *On the Road* royalties. He was soon bored and traveled alone to Mexico City where he stayed for a few months working on the first draft of what would become *Desolation Angels*, which he'd begun years earlier.

He was in Lowell in 1962 for the publication of *Big Sur*, and then went to see John Clellon Holmes in Old Saybrook, Connecticut. For Holmes it was an tumultuous visit. When Kerouac was gone, he noted in his diary that Jack, "although sweet and tentative when sober becomes truculent, paranoid, garrulous, stiff-jointed, wild-eyed, exhaustless and amnesiac when drunk. Booze alone can seem to produce in him the 'ecstasy' he needs to get through time. . . . Way down deep, I think, he wants to die, and no amount of self-abuse, disaster or sadness can expunge the feeling of loss and estrangement which has always scarred him, dogged him, driven him."

*Big Sur* was savaged by the reviewers. And Jack was ridiculed by *Time*'s anonymous hatchet person: "A child's first touch of cold mortality — even when it occurs in a man of 41 — may seem ridiculous, and is certainly pathetic." As if "cold mortality" hadn't been Kerouac's main concern, his obsession, since the death of his brother in 1926.

Back on Long Island, he reconnected with the painter Stanley Twardowicz, who would be a drinking buddy and confidant for the rest of Jack's life. Kerouac had a teenage girlfriend named Yseult who at his urging called him Tristan. He occasionally managed to escape from his mother and flee to the city where, when unable to find a willing woman, he pleaded with Ginsberg and Peter Orlovsky for sexual favors.

In 1963, Neal Cassady showed up at his door in Northport, but the visit was not a success. They weren't able to communicate as before.

*Visions of Gerard* came out in September, 1963, and got the usual terrible reviews, being called "self-indulgent" and "grossly sentimental." These notices hurt Kerouac more than all others because the book was sacred to him. The *New York Times* accused him of "debasing" his dead brother's suffering with his "garrulous hipster yawping."

A few months later, Kerouac was invited to speak at Lowell House at Harvard University. He was so impressed that, against his better judgment, he accepted. He shared quarters with Al Gelpi, the professor who had invited him. Gelpi remembered that Kerouac was so nervous during the two days leading up to the talk that he went from bar to bar downing boilermakers and sketching pietàs on coasters. What he had to say to the students resembled nothing they wanted to hear. He spoke for Jesus and against Chairman Mao. The students booed. The senior tutor passed Gelpi a note telling him to get this guy out of here. Kerouac's reaction was to recite Emily Dickinson.

The next day the *Harvard Crimson* labeled him a "clown."

In September 1964, the Long Island paper *Newsday* sent a writer named Val Duncan to Northport to see what the King of the Beats was doing. Duncan found Jack in his living-room rocking chair, bare feet in red slippers, needing a shave but with startlingly blue eyes. He had a can of beer in one hand and a shot glass in the other.

Kerouac took the reporter to his room where the shelves were lined with "a thousand books, from Allen Ginsberg to Aristophanes." Kerouac went to the precise middle of the floor, stood on his head, lowered and raised his feet ten times. Duncan noted the "rippling muscles" of a stomach "hard as a butcher's block" and "without an ounce of fat."

Kerouac put jazz on the hi-fi, then switched to Shostakovich, danced around the room, suddenly stopped, and began to cry, pleading with Duncan, "Listen to the pain and sweetness of it."

He was currently working on a book about his childhood called *Memory Babe*.

When the interview was over, Kerouac asked Duncan for a ride downtown. The reporter dropped him off at a bar. "He shuffles inside, shirttail flapping, still in his tattered slippers. He doesn't know what will happen next and doesn't seem to care."

His mother cared and wanted to get him out of Northport and down to Florida, ostensibly to put some distance between him and bad influences. She would also be near her daughter. But Kerouac would have nothing to do with Orlando. In 1963, he had tried to collect some money from Nin's husband, who owed him thousands of dollars. When his brother-in-law refused to repay him, Kerouac made a scene, and Nin called the cops, who escorted Jack to Orlando airport.

So Jack and his mother compromised on St. Petersburg. When all his Northport friends, same as all his friends everywhere else, told him he shouldn't be so attached to Mémère, Kerouac repeated once more that he had made a vow to his father to take care of his mother.

He sold the house in Northport, bought one in St. Petersburg, and, in the meantime, fled to the city for a rendezvous with Neal and his new main companion, Ken Kesey. Kerouac arrived at an apartment filled with expensive electronic equipment, floors covered with cables, lights flashing, rock and roll blaring, tape reels turning. Jack was disappointed with the hardness he saw in Neal; he didn't like Kesey, hated the music, and felt no empathy with the ill-mannered kids with long hair and bare feet. It seemed to him as if everyone was posing, playing a role; nobody was being sincere. Allen Ginsberg was there, of course, and draped Jack with the American flag. Over the years, the story of this encounter would evolve until Kerouac became a drunken, short-haired, right-wing bore who remonstrated with the long-haired enlightened while sloppily refolding his precious flag. In photos, however, he looks fresh-faced and well-combed, and in each picture the flag is around his shoulders like a shawl.

None of the commentators — whether Merry Pranksters, Allen Ginsberg, or the novelist Robert Stone — on this "epic" encounter between Kerouac, the old guard, and Kesey, the vanguard, with Neal the liaison seem to even consider the possibility that Kerouac did not find them interesting. There is, indeed, no evidence that any of these people could conceive of the fact that they were not interesting. You were either on the bus or you were off the bus. If you were under thirty it might have been an adventure. If you were, on the other hand, a grown-up, you probably had to be on the hustle to be on the bus.

Kerouac wasn't well-combed a week later, when he went to Fire Island for a few days, wandered the beaches, and got arrested. Back in Northport, the night before he was to leave for Florida, Kerouac went with his mother to a going-away party hosted by Stanley Twardowicz. Jack disappeared in the wee hours, and was found two days later asleep in a field outside of town.

# The Long Slow Death of Jack Kerouac 59

Cliff Anderson met the King of the Beats not long after Jack moved to St. Pete. Cliff was in the habit, when he got off work at midnight, of walking across the street for a drink at a place called the Tic Toc. The bathroom at the Tic Toc was at the back, just past the pool table. Cliff had noticed some guys playing pool, particularly "one real rough-looking dude," who was wearing blue serge trousers with a hole in the seat, the bottoms rolled up, and a red elastic belt so long that the buckle dragged along the floor. When Anderson headed for the bathroom, the guy put the touch on him for a quarter.

Later, the man came walking along the line of drinkers at the bar and went to the front door. Cliff had sort of hunkered down to make himself as inconspicuous as possible under the circumstances. The guy "looked like a real bum," and Anderson didn't want to get hit up again. When the man reached the door, he "did a sort of double take" and came back, Cliff thinking, "Oh, no."

The man thanked him for the quarter, said he'd pay it back, and introduced himself as Jack Kerouac. Cliff laughed, not believing him for an instant. The man insisted. Cliff, who'd read Kerouac, began asking him questions, "What did Doctor Sax say when. . ." or "In *Big Sur*, who is Billy?"

The guy got many of the questions wrong and told Cliff, "Gee, you know my work better than I do."

Cliff laughed at that and told him, if he was Jack Kerouac, he could speak French. But Cliff didn't understand French so he had no way of knowing whether the guy had begun spouting gibberish or what. Still, he was intrigued if not convinced. So when Cliff's buddy showed up with his Triumph convertible, they all went out together and got big bottles of wine. The friend hung in for twenty-four hours, and Cliff got his '51 Chevy to drive the bum home. It wasn't until he saw "Jack Kerouac" on the mailbox that he became a believer.

The author went to his bedroom and came back waving a twenty-dollar bill. Anderson and Kerouac proceeded to go on a fifteen-day drinking spree, Jack returning home every couple of days, just long enough to get another twenty.

Cliff would become Jack's best friend, his closest of the later years. Kerouac was wary of everyone he met who'd heard of him, leery of sycophants, afraid of personal attacks, and, most of all, he abhorred literary discussions. People would show up at his house or approach him in bars, demanding he pose with them for photographs. Strangers accosted Kerouac at parties to point out shortcomings in his work. But Cliff Anderson was a tough young kid who'd read a lot, could shoot pool, and was still hanging in after the first few bottles.

Cliff chose with discretion the people he would introduce to Jack. One of these was Carl Adkins. They got together on New Year's Eve, 1965, and Adkins thought Kerouac looked "rugged, bearish like a hockey player."

That night, they headed for a party at a rented hall on the beach where Adkins learned, immediately, that the ingredients for disaster consisted of Kerouac and a crowd, "any crowd."

Adkins was standing with Kerouac when a man came up and introduced his wife to Jack, saying that she was from Paris. They started speaking French and almost immediately began to scream at each other. Two people screaming led to other people hollering, and to fights breaking out. Cliff and Carl managed to get Kerouac out of there, and by the time police arrived, they were laughing about it at an all-night diner in St. Pete.

The main attraction at this place, a White Tower, was the guy who worked behind the counter, John. He was, in Adkins' term, "a beanery madman." He juggled plates, made change, cleaned the grill with a spatula, flipped pancakes with one hand and scrambled eggs with the other, and all the while Kerouac applauded, shouting, "Go, John, go!"

"When Jack felt good," Adkins remembers, "he could generate happiness as effortlessly as a Cadillac battery could fire up the bulb in a flashlight."

Many people remark that Kerouac would make provocative statements or utter insults to break down people's reserve or hypocrisy, or just to get things happening. He seemed to enjoy people calling him out on his comments. One night, Larry Vickers came into the Wild Boar, a bar run by Gerry Wagner, an ex-professor at SFU. Larry was in his "Sears-Roebuck suit," accompanied by his wife Renee, having just come from a dreary local opera. When Wagner introduced him, Kerouac said, "Well, isn't he the pretty one."

"Fuck you, Kerouac," Vickers replied.

Kerouac laughed and they became friends. That night Vickers and his wife drove Kerouac and some others to Wagner's home on the lake to drink wine. The six-foot-four-inch, two-hundred-and-forty-pound Wagner was a great friend to Kerouac. They were fond of "belly busting," sticking out their stomachs and running into each other.

When Kerouac was in town, usually accompanied by Cliff Anderson, the drinking would last for three or four days. "We'd try to handle Jack in shifts," said Vickers, "with one or two people sleeping while one or two stayed awake to drink and talk with him, or simply listen to him go into long monologues."

Part of Kerouac's magic, Vickers thought, was that "he held the key to a heaven in which none of us really believed."

Nick Lowe, a local musician, was taking a break between sets at a joint in St. Pete when an acquaintance told him to come over to the bar because "Jack Kerouac's there."

He saw a middle-aged man in a T-shirt and baggy pants who was telling a story and didn't want to be interrupted. Lowe couldn't believe it was Jack Kerouac because the famous author would surely be more impressive. After the last set, he went to the bar for a drink; the guy was still talking, and Lowe, with his musician's ear, became curious about the sound of the man's voice. After a while, the guy turned and asked him for a ride home. Later he seemed surprised when Lowe refused his offer of a few bucks for gas. The man said, "Well, come on in and listen to some good music."

Inside, Lowe saw the books and photos, and knew it really was Kerouac. They would eventually spend a lot of time together. Lowe confirms what other friends would say, that Kerouac liked you if you didn't fawn over him.

Many times, Kerouac was there for Lowe's final set, after which they'd head off for more drinking or go for breakfast, often to see John the grill man.

Lowe criticizes those biographers who say that Kerouac in those years "was tired and burned out . . . they didn't have to try to keep up with him."

Lowe might drop Kerouac off at three in the morning and drive home only to be woken at dawn by a knock on the door. There would be Kerouac, who'd turn to wave the cabbie away: "You can go now. My friend's here."

Lowe maintains that Kerouac's "downfall" was his "empathetic openness to the pain and suffering" he encountered everywhere. "I've never seen such tenderness in a grown man."

In May 1965, there was a new book, *Desolation Angels*, and perhaps to absent himself when the predictable scathing reviews appeared, but ostensibly to pursue genealogical research, Kerouac flew to France.

Before he left, Adkins ran into him waiting for a bus downtown. He was on an errand concerning his passport. Kerouac said he was in his traveling outfit: crepe-soled shoes, khaki slacks, an old belt "that would go around his waist twice," and a shirt "that looked as if it would glow in the dark."

Jack had indicated he'd probably be gone for months, so Cliff and some of the others took a trip to Mexico. When they got back in four or five weeks, they discovered Jack had not only made his trip but written *Satori in Paris*, a minor masterpiece.

In Paris and Brittany, instead of finding the truth about his family past, Kerouac discovered — or, rather, reaffirmed — his belief in the connectedness of all people. Hence, the Buddhist word in the title of this most Catholic of books. From the outset, he states his purpose is to convey reverence for life. Kerouac was courageous enough to portray himself as a bumbling goof, all the better to allow the reader to laugh at him and thereby relax his or her defenses and preconceived notions, and be open for this humble but important truth. Here Kerouac is a universal pilgrim, a Buddhist bound for Bodh Gaya, Hindi for Mount Arunachala; he's pudgy Silenus muttering Catholic haikus and hugging the wine jug; he's the Ghost of the Susquehanna, a gypsy girl at the Cathedral of Notre Dame, a drunken Canuck with rosary beads and Buddhist prayer beads in his baggage, going nowhere.

Having accomplished his real purpose, Kerouac wanted to get home to Florida to see, as he writes in *Satori*, Cliff Anderson, his pool shooting buddy, and to get his "ribs in Winn-Dixie, dear God."

He talked Cliff and a guy called Paddy Mitchell into driving him to Lowell. They set off in Cliff's '51 Chevy, Jack ad-libbing the blues while Paddy played harmonica. Kerouac wanted to call at every bar on highway 301. Near the Georgia line, stopped at a railroad crossing, Kerouac jumped out of the Chevy, raced for the freight, hopped on an open boxcar, rode it a couple hundred yards, jumped off, and sprinted back to the car.

They didn't pause until Chapel Hill, where a hitchhiker announced Kerouac's presence in a bar and precipitated a party that came to resemble a riot. The next morning they were off to Connecticut for three days to visit with John Clellon Holmes. Then it was on to Lowell, where Jack took them to the Sampas home for spinach pie, and Cliff met Stella for the first time. Wanting to stay around awhile, Jack gave Cliff and Paddy expense money and they left immediately for Florida. That same night Kerouac was arrested in Lowell for being drunk and disorderly.

Jack went to Albany, New York, with Tony Sampas and made friends with a psychiatrist named Danny De Sole. He was reunited with Al Gelpi and met Al's brother, Don, a Jesuit priest. One evening at a party, Kerouac envisioned a Catholic saint watching over each person in the room. He proceeded to tell the story of the saint and its relation to each person. Don Gelpi was so astounded by this display that he mentioned it in his book *Experiencing God.*

Kerouac's mother wanted to move back to Massachusetts, so Jack put the St. Pete house on the market and bought a split-level home in a middle-class neighborhood of Hyannis, where his main companion was the black novelist Robert Boles.

Having been invited to Italy, Jack was afraid of going and making a fool of himself. But, desperately needing the money, he flew to Europe at the end of September 1966. He knocked back Scotch all the way to London and had to be helped off the plane. An airline representative telephoned Kerouac's Milan publisher — Mondadori — and the idiot who got on the line told the author, "Don't make a fool of yourself."

When Kerouac reached Milan, the publisher had a

doctor on hand to sedate him and give him morphine. They locked him in a hotel room, but television host Nanda Pivano came to his aid and brought Kerouac to her home. The publisher's people were repelled because he looked like a proletarian.

After Pivano interviewed him on television, the Mondadori people set Kerouac on the Italian road with their representative, Domenico Porzio. They went to Naples and on the return trip stopped in Rome. There Kerouac was profiled in *l'Espresso* magazine by Alberto Arbasino, after which Porzio took him to lunch at Il Bolognese, a fashionable restaurant in Piazza del Popolo.

Giulia Niccolai was hanging around outside the Rosati, a bar next door to the restaurant, when a cab pulled up and Porzio and Kerouac got out. Niccolai recognized Kerouac immediately from pictures. Niccolai was thirty-three years old, had just published her first novel, and moved easily through the cultural scene in Rome. She had met Gregory Corso a few years earlier and found him as comfortable as an old pal from school. She'd spent time with Yevtushenko and couldn't stand him. With Kerouac, however, she was in awe.

Porzio, she would recall, had the appearance of a worn-out lion tamer. Knowing Niccolai spoke English, he invited her to lunch with them. Kerouac wasn't drunk, although he'd had a couple. He didn't relax the entire two hours, spent his time looking around and looking irritated. It was exactly the kind of place not to take Jack Kerouac, being filled, as Niccolai indicated, with pretentious writers and movie people. He didn't hold back his opinions, which she dutifully

# The Long Slow Death of Jack Kerouac 67

translated. Simultaneously, Niccolai studied Jack to see how he coincided with his writings, and realized that he did, all the way and "absolutely."

A couple of weeks after returning to Hyannis, Jack married Stella Sampas, who was four years older than him, and sister of his adolescent buddy Sebastian. Stella had, evidently, been in love with Jack since those early Lowell years when he had come to the house to visit Sebastian. For Jack it was, frankly, a marriage of convenience. His mother was now partially paralyzed and he needed someone to help take care of her.

They moved into a large split-level house on Sanders Avenue in the exclusive area of Lowell. In March 1967, Kerouac began a new version of *Vanity of Duluoz*, subtitled *An Adventurous Education*, about his years of early manhood. On the very first page, he succinctly recorded his view of life, and the book amounts to a beautiful yet self-parodying poem to hope and disillusionment.

That spring a film crew from Montreal came to Lowell on a project about French-Canadians in New England. They took their cameras into the Pawtucketville Social Club, and there was Kerouac shooting pool with the other guys. The best of Kerouac's biographers, Gerry Nicosia, writes that every time the camera was on him, Jack yelled, "Fuck you!" I have seen the film several times, and this simply is not so. In fact, the film hardly emphasizes him and the most noteworthy thing about the footage is that he seems to stand out while at the same time fitting right in with all the others, just normal small-town workingmen. If the only ones for him were those who burned like fabulous Roman candles and never said a commonplace thing, these weren't them. Jack was there but wasn't there, which was also true of him at a Greenwich Village poetry reading, in an old car crossing the great plains, a ship's mess, or a circle of Buddhists at a Marin County cabin — and it is also, as the saying goes, the story of his life.

Jack was invited by Radio-Canada to come to Montreal and appear as a guest on the television interview show *Sel de la semaine*. Here he definitely does not fit in, looking like a truck driver from the Chicoutimi surrounded by office workers from the Place Ville Marie. But they are friendly office workers, if a little in awe of the guest. They do not, as Nicosia says, laugh at Kerouac. They laugh with his jokes, non sequiturs, and deadpan hilarious responses to serious questions. Furthermore, Nicosia's statement that the "Québecois" had never heard anything like his "quaint Pawtucketville phrasing" is absurd. He spoke French like that truck driver from Chicoutimi or Cheticamp, in the Acadian area of Nova Scotia's Cape Breton, or like all the characters of *la pègre* — the underworld — that you come across in the area around Pie IX metro stop in the east end of Montreal.

The summer of 1967, while thousands of North Americans, mainly college kids, along with drug dealers, the FBI, and would-be gurus like Allen Ginsberg, were heading for San Francisco with flowers in their hair, Kerouac with bottles of Scotch was being driven by Joe Chaput to Rivière du Loup to look for traces of his ancestry. What he found was mostly barrooms.

He allowed himself to be dragged to Europe by two

of his brothers-in-law and some of their friends. Of all Kerouac's trips, this is the one about which the least is known. None of the participants are talking. It has been suggested that they brought Jack along because they thought it would be a laugh to watch him cavort. If so, they evidently got more than they could handle. He disappeared in Copenhagen; in Lisbon, he carried on with the kind of whores even other whores shunned; in Madrid, he disappeared; in Stuttgart, after seeing the German army march by on parade, he locked himself in his hotel room, refusing to come out, crying for hours and hours with guilt for all the anti-Semitic trash he'd ever spoken. His companions left him in the hotel room and flew back to Lowell. Two weeks later, Kerouac showed up. Where he'd been and what he'd been doing no one ever discovered.

Early in 1968, a few days after the publication of *Vanity of Duluoz*, Kerouac learned that Neal Cassady had died of exposure on a stretch of railroad track outside San Miguel de Allende in Mexico. That night, Kerouac was arrested on the streets of Lowell for drunk and disorderly, and for disturbing the peace.

He continued to hit the bars, cause trouble, make merry, and make mayhem. Twenty-five years after Kerouac's death, when a writer and a photographer came to Lowell from Italy to do a book on Jack's town, they found that to most of the citizens, he was a bum. Which just proves what happens to someone who leaves Lowell, thinking they're better than everyone else. "Maybe he was a great writer," said a Lowell storekeeper. "But for us he was a drunk. And quite frankly we were embarrassed by his lifestyle."

One day, walking on Central Avenue, he went into the Lowell Pet Shop to play with the puppies, and was moved to buy them all. He took them home in boxes in a taxi. Stella made him send them back.

Graham Cournoyer remembers that despite all his madcap adventures, "Jack was a poor lonely fucker."

Brian Foye, who grew up in Lowell, remembers the Kerouac of 1968, "walking up Walker Avenue in the early evenings — short jacket, baseball cap, head down — an overwhelmingly lonely figure."

Another Lowell resident told the Italians, "We asked Kerouac, 'If you're such a famous writer, how come you ended up like this?'"

The *Boston Globe* sent around a reporter named Gregory McDonald to find out what the King of the Beats was doing in his exile from a cultural scene that he, more than anyone, had originated. The writer found a desperate man he thought in need of help, and was appalled that no one around Kerouac seemed to realize his trouble, much less come to his aid.

Yet, a couple of weeks later when Ted Berrigan arrived in Lowell, dispatched for the *Paris Review*, the Kerouac he interviewed was brilliant and idiosyncratic. Poets Aram Saroyan and Duncan McNaughton had come along, and Saroyan later wrote that they encountered a man who was thoroughly open and sensitive, everything that his generation only talked about being.

Kerouac was invited to appear on William F. Buckley's pseudo-intellectual TV talk show, *The Firing Line*. The theme was the hippie movement and its origins. Jack didn't want to accept, but shrewd Mémère reminded

## The Long Slow Death of Jack Kerouac 71

him that the exposure would be good for *Vanity of Duluoz*, which wasn't selling. Joe Chaput was his chauffeur to New York. Brother-in-law Nick and a Lowell friend, ex-prizefighter Billy Koums, went along. Jack drank all the way to New York, drank all night at a bar run by Lowellite and former light heavyweight boxing champ Billy Conn, and drank until daylight with Lucien Carr. And then he drank all day until showtime. When he got to the studio, he saw Truman Capote getting made up for another show. Capote — who in reference to Kerouac's work had uttered the famous line, "That's not writing, it's typing" — was terrified. But Kerouac offered his hand, saying he harbored no bad feelings.

Kerouac's appearance on *The Firing Line*, along with Ed Sanders of the Fugs and sociologist Lewis Yablonsky, is always reviewed as being a complete and utter disaster. It is said — and said over and over again — that Kerouac came off like a fat and tired redneck muttering right-wing obscenities in the rare moments he was coherent. Well, he did have a belly, but the rest of it is nonsense. The criticisms have been made by products of the generation that is identified by the Sixties. People who came of age protesting the war in Vietnam, worshipping people like John Lennon, chanting shibboleths, and following anyone in a robe just off a 747 from the East. Looks were extremely important to this generation and Kerouac didn't look like its idea of anything but a redneck. Something that generation was not famous for is having a sense of humor, so when Kerouac says the war in Vietnam is a plot to get jeeps into the country, it's his way of sending up the smugness of the questions. Or, as Ginsberg said, "He didn't give a shit about TV or the sacredness of the occasion."

Kerouac was bored, half drunk, and half asleep, yet still could outquip Buckley; at one point, without Buckley realizing it, Kerouac even mimicked his self-satisfied drawl. When you were on Buckley's show you were supposed to show respect, acknowledge the great honor and responsibility engraved in the invitation. But Kerouac finally turned his back on the host, calling to Sanders, "Hey, Ed. I got arrested two weeks ago. The arresting officer said he was bringing me in for 'Decay'! Hah!"

Earlier, when Sanders wondered, disingenuously, why Russians and Americans couldn't just dance around together, holding hands and covered with strawberry jam, Kerouac asked, "Can I lick you?"

Not long after the show, Kerouac moved back to St. Pete, to a house on Tenth Avenue just a few blocks from the old one. And again Joe Chaput drove him, along with Stella and Mémère on mattresses in the back of the station wagon. Chaput remembered that "Jack talked and drank all the way down. Talked and drank. Never stopped. God, he was great."

After Joe headed north, Jack connected with Cliff Anderson and they went to a house in the woods and took LSD. They continued to see each other, but it wasn't quite the same as before. "Jack was a married man now," Cliff recalls. He didn't get a telephone until the last days, and if Cliff came over unannounced, the door often opened onto a depressing scene: the mother, bedridden in one room, Stella taking care of

## The Long Slow Death of Jack Kerouac 73

her, Jack feeling guilty for not being able to do more, and leery of going out, getting drunk, and upsetting the domestic situation even further. But still there were visits. "Other people have written about what a bummer he was on in that period, but it's just not true," Cliff maintains. "We had a great time. We had a ball."

Kerouac wrote an essay for the *Boston Globe* called "After Me, the Deluge," a summation of his position in regard to the current cultural and political situation. It is really a brilliant work of satire — satire being another thing that went unappreciated by most of that generation around which our notions of the Sixties have coalesced. The piece went into syndication and was picked up by the *Miami Herald*, which sent a staff writer, Jack McClintock, to prepare an accompanying profile of Kerouac.

McClintock pushed aside palm fronds to knock at the door. Stella told him Jack wasn't there. Then an unshaven man appeared behind her and told him to come in. Kerouac was barefoot, wearing a yellow-and-brown sport shirt opened over an inside-out T-shirt. "I'm glad to see you," he told McClintock, "'cause I'm so lonesome here."

The television was on with no sound, Handel's *Messiah* booming from the hi-fi.

Self-conscious about his appearance and his belly, Kerouac added, "I'm dressed like this because I have a bad hernia." His navel hernia was so extreme it was secured with a half-dollar kept in place by adhesive tape.

It was the first of a dozen visits by McClintock in these last few months of Kerouac's life. By the author's chair was a table that invariably held books — usually classics — issues of *National Review*, cans of beer, and medicine vials filled with Scotch.

McClintock found Kerouac to be the ideal conversationalist and drinking companion: witty, erudite, and funny. Sometimes Kerouac read his work out loud or assumed accents, spontaneously invented scenarios, performances that were astonishing to the reporter and the selected friends he brought around.

One day, Kerouac announced that he had just finished another book, a real novel this time. It was about a ten-year-old black boy whose name derived from the old *Pictorial Review Magazine*. The novel was called *Pic*. When one of McClintock's friends asked him if it was about prejudice and the racial situation, Kerouac answered, "No, it's about life."

Shortly after that visit, Kerouac, in the company of a disabled Vietnam veteran, went to the Cactus, a rough black bar, and they were not welcome. It has been written that Kerouac was so out of touch that he thought he could go into a place like that in those racially tense times and not be hassled. Or, maybe, having just finished a tender story about a black boy rescued by his big brother, Kerouac was seeking a sense of connection.

The men, seeing how Kerouac's buddy walked, began to taunt, calling him a faggot and pushing him around. Kerouac attempted to intervene, saying, "He's crippled, he's not queer."

Then the men turned their attention on Jack and the other guy slipped out the door. Kerouac was knocked to the ground and kicked repeatedly. Finally, they dragged him outside and kicked him some more — beat him, in fact, until he was unconscious.

Sometime later, a cruising police car found Kerouac crawling across the pavement. Rather than take him to the hospital, the police hauled him downtown to jail. After all, he was a known rowdy and drunk, and they'd picked him up several times before. Some hours later, Stella, driven by a neighbor, came downtown to bail him out. Jack's clothes were covered in blood, his eyes were swollen, and he was still bleeding from a gash in his forehead. He stumbled out holding his stomach. The neighbor drove them to the emergency room at St. Anthony's hospital. Kerouac's head wound required nine stitches; he had three broken ribs and allowed his chest to be taped. The examining physician told Kerouac his hernia was severe and advised him to stay in the hospital to have it taken care of. As well, he was bleeding internally. Kerouac refused further treatment.

A week later, Kerouac wrote to Edie Parker that he had suffered a very bad beating in a bar.

He slept with pillows under his thighs and upper chest to protect his ribs and stomach. He spent most days in the backyard, lying on a lounge chair that Stella had bought with Green Stamps. At night, he wanted her to lie out there with him and look at the heavens. "He told me all about the stars," she later said.

On October 14, Jack McClintock came to visit and found Kerouac to be "extra cheerful." His injuries had frightened him into drinking less, and he was much thinner. Kerouac bragged about losing twenty pounds. In this, their last conversation, the talk ranged over writers and writing, painting, women, music, and football.

On the eighteenth, Cliff Anderson came around for a few hours. Cliff remembers Jack waving goodbye.

The next evening, Jack had a visit from Al Ellis, a law student he'd met through McClintock. Jack took Al into the kitchen and showed him the new phone on the wall. Kerouac also had a new phone book in which there were no more than half a dozen numbers, each one circled, each one local.

That night he spent on his lounge chair in the yard.

The morning of the twentieth, he sat down in front of the television with the sound off, the hi-fi on, eating tuna fish and taking notes for a new novel, set around his father's printing and vaudeville activities, to be called *Spotlight Print*.

It has been said and often repeated that the King of the Beats took fatally sick while watching *The Galloping Gourmet* on television. A good story except for the fact that it wasn't on that day.

Stella found him on his knees in the bathroom, vomiting blood. While waiting for the ambulance, Jack telephoned Nick Lowe. "I have to go to the hospital," he said. "It must be the damned tuna fish."

At St. Anthony's he was given numerous blood transfusions, but they were unable to save him. Kerouac died at 5 AM, on October 21.

Over the years, Kerouac had told a few people that he wanted to die but couldn't commit suicide because he was a Catholic. He intended, therefore, to drink himself to death. But he also told people he was Tristan and Lancelot in former lives and Kerouac was the name of one of the nations of the Iroquois, and that he remembered the day before he was born.

Perhaps Kerouac did want to take, as the old bluesmen used to say, the shortcut home. And drinking was the path. But he hadn't been ready just yet. It was a bar beating that got him home quicker than intended, and safe in heaven dead.

# SIX

I did not know where I entered
But when I saw myself there,
Not knowing where I entered,
Many things I suddenly learned;
I will not say what these things were,
For I remained not knowing,
*Beyond all science knowing.*

It was peace, it was love,
It was the perfect knowledge,
In deep loneliness I saw with wisdom;
It was a thing so secret
I was left babbling and trembling,
*Beyond all science knowing.*

— St. John of the Cross

"Kerouac, it seems, was born knowing."
— William Burroughs

Jack Kerouac was a religious writer and an alien. Reviewing his life and work now, after all these years of thinking I knew it, has emphasized these obvious truths. Like so many other Kerouac readers, I would always have granted that his profound longing was saturated with religious — Catholic or Buddhist —

reference and terminology. Likewise, and particularly as a Canadian, I was aware of the importance of his French-Canadian heritage, his portrayal of Lowell childhood being similar to the Quebec childhoods drawn — with less power, it must be said — by Francophone writers. I certainly realized that Kerouac's acute sensitivity to the English language derived from his hearing it as an exotic tongue, and I have recently discovered a letter Kerouac wrote in 1951 to Franco-American journalist Yvonne Le Maître, in which he emphasizes, "All my knowledge rests in my 'French-Canadianness' and nowhere else."

But what I understand now is that the religion in Kerouac's books is not incidental and that he remained an immigrant.

His first novel, *The Town and the City*, is as much a Quebec-emigrant story as it is a Wolfean American family epic. Kerouac shrewdly calls his family the Martins, a French name that, on the page, appears perfectly American. Although the father of the clan is Anglo-Saxon, the mother, Marguerite, is French-Canadian. The novel was published in 1950, two years after the Quebec publication of Roger Lemelin's *Les Plouffe*, generally acknowledged as the work that started a revolution in Quebec literature.

*Les Plouffe*, published in the rest of Canada in English in 1952, was the second of a series, between *Au pied de la pente douce* (*The Town Below*) in 1944 and *Pierre le magnifique* (*In Quest of Splendour*) in 1952. Together they portray the recent cracks in an historically insular society and a new Quebec that is beginning to emerge.

*The Town Below* resembles those first pages of Kerouac's book when he is giving an overview of Lowell — called Galloway — just like Thornton Wilder does in *Our Town* — and before he focuses on the Martin clan.

*In Quest of Splendour* is a story of the romantic inner pilgrimage of a young man who rejects and then accepts his religious inclinations. Had Kerouac been born in Quebec and never left, this is the kind of book he might have written.

But it is *The Plouffe Family*, the middle work of Lemelin's series, that *The Town and the City* most resembles.

Both are stories of large French-Canadian families in which the father is a printer and the mother rules the house. In both novels, family members work in shoe factories, and baseball and bicycles are mentioned in the very first pages. *The Town and the City* covers the years 1935 to 1945; *The Plouffe Family*, 1938 to 1945; and the father dies at the end of each novel. (And there is an "old man Plouffe" in *Doctor Sax*.)

But Lemelin's tone is ironic, satirical; his interest is less in the members of the Plouffe family as individuals than the society that formed them and in which they struggle. What emerges from the cracks in the society will not abandon it. None of the boys, neither Ovide, Napoleon, nor Guillaume are destined to hit the road. There is no place to go. They are Quebec.

At the end of *The Town and the City*, Peter Martin, the child most like Jack Kerouac, turns up his collar and strides off into the rain, the voices in his head asking where he's going. There is no answer. There wasn't an answer for Kerouac. He was of no country, a wandering *bhikkhu*, a *voltigeur*, a seeker on a permanent pilgrimage.

Two entirely different generations are responsible for Kerouac's reputation and neither grasped what he was really about. Kerouac came of literary age when the arbiters were products of the cynical, smirking Twenties. "That generation forms the corpus of our authority today," Kerouac wrote, "and is looking with disfavor upon us, under beetling brows, at us who want to swing — in life, in art, in everything."

That generation was itself a reaction against the turbulent literary modernism that flamed in the teens of the century and was snuffed out by the First World War. The new literary heroes — Fitzgerald, Hemingway, Sinclair Lewis — were all products of small-town American middle-class life. They didn't even bother to shoot the usual youthful rubber bullets at convention but instead went abroad for their flings, and returned simultaneously smug and guilty about foreign peccadillos, to assume their places in the cultural Establishment.

After the Second World War, most of America was hell-bent for the suburbs. Papa Hemingway was every ad man's hero and Jack Kerouac and the Beat Generation represented a tidal wave in their martini glasses.

Reviewers completely misunderstood — or maliciously distorted — Kerouac's books, putting him in a lineup of greasy delinquents that included James Dean and Marlon Brando and Elvis Presley, and accused him of promoting a switchblade attack on American values. This was the position not only of hack pop commentators but of supposedly serious reviewers. For once the WASPs of television and advertising in New York were united with what Allen Ginsberg called "professional Jewish literary critics," to defame and demean Kerouac and himself. After Norman Podhoretz wrote his scathing and infamous Beat putdown, "The Know-Nothing Bohemians," calling Kerouac an agent of criminality, he approached Ginsberg at a party and told him, "You know, you could have a career in New York in publishing if you'd get rid of Kerouac."

But as Thomas Merton commentated at the time, "Squares need Beats in order to feel virtuous."

Kerouac was also like Elvis in that he was dangerously good-looking. Yet, he was primarily — as a 1958 article he wrote was titled — a "Lamb, No Lion." He said that with every book he made a supplication to the Lord, and he meant it. And who the hell knew what to make of that or him? There had never been anything like him.

They beat up on Kerouac for a few years and then they ignored him. At the end, his books weren't selling. His total income for the ten months of 1969 that he got to live was $2,000. His wife was taking in sewing. When he died, Kerouac had sixty-two dollars in the bank.

No sooner was he dead than a fight began over his estate. A week before he died, he wrote a letter to his nephew Paul Blake in Alaska stating his intention to divorce Stella and leave everything to him and Mémère, and that he wanted the Sampases to get nothing from him. In a four-hour phone conversation with Edie Parker, shortly after the beating at the Cactus, Jack said he feared he might die of his injuries. But if he lived, he wanted to remarry her. Edie told him that a legal case might be made that they were still married because she'd been advised that their annulment was not valid.

In relating this conversation to me, Edie Parker swore Jack was not drunk when they talked. Some of what she claims is in a letter Jack wrote to her in October 1969, and which hopefully will be published in the second volume of his letters (although that's probably a faint hope, given that the estate did not, in volume one — to 1956 — permit to be published any letters Kerouac wrote to wives or girlfriends). Stella lived until 1989, during which time she permitted only *Visions of Cody* to appear. Stella, and her brothers after her, liked to pretend there was nothing, save for Jack's Buddhist meditations, *Some of the Dharma*, that remained unpublished. Stella told me exactly this in a phone conversation in 1977. She was still living in the house where Jack died, and the number was still listed in his name. "There is nothing but some poems," she said. "And all his notebooks, but there's nothing worthwhile in them. You know, I'm a writer too."

Yet everyone who knew Kerouac was aware of many unpublished books, as well as shorter and incomplete works, such as several hundreds of pages of the childhood novel *Memory Babe*.

In 1951, Kerouac wrote, in French, a novella called *La nuit est ma femme*. One single page of this work appeared to much fanfare in *La nouvelle revue française* in the summer of 1996.

Jack's daughter, Jan Michelle Kerouac, was unsuccessful in asserting her claim to at least a share in the estate. She died of leukemia in 1996.

One commentator, Brian Foye, who was instrumental in having the monument erected to Jack in Lowell — although his plans were co-opted by typical civic machinations — wrote that the Sampases are "like an organism reacting to constant negative impulses, drawing back like an ethnic mill family."

In the late Seventies, *Heart Beat* was released, based on a memoir by Carolyn Cassady. Nick Nolte played a lugubrious Neal, John Heard a maundering Jack, and Sissy Spacek a giggling airhead Carolyn. Only after filming did Sissy Spacek read *Heart Beat*, and when she met Carolyn, broke into tears over what had been done. The movie *Heart Beat* makes the movie *The Subterraneans* look like an enduring classic.

Kerouac has been ill-served by his numerous biographers. The first biography, *Kerouac*, by Ann Charters, appeared a year after his death, and it is the worst. The author does little more than arrange the novels chronologically and insert real names. Charters completely disregards the last years of Kerouac's life, with the exception of her own visit to him in 1966. Other than Gerald Nicosia, in his biography *Memory Babe*, all biographers virtually ignore his last decade. An English book, *Angelheaded Hipster*, by Steve Turner, was published in 1996, and has good pictures. Otherwise, Nicosia's is the only biography worth a look, and that look should be under eyebrows raised high as they'll go.

In the Fifties, Kerouac was viewed from the perspective of a cynical crowd shaped by middle-class heroes of a lost generation. His reputation was later revised by biographers who, with the exception of

Ann Charters, are products of the consciousness of the media phenomenon of the Sixties, which had less to do with the actual decade than with a mass-media-co-opted rebellion of middle-class youth. No matter how sincere participants in the Sixties may have been, the notions of Peace, Love, and Revolution were appropriated and provided with concomitant heroes and villains. Not the least of the selling jobs was the taking of a simplistic, status quo youth music — rock and roll — and packaging it as the soundtrack of Revolution.

Biographers formed by this mindset, but who had discovered Kerouac somewhere along the line, were attracted by the notion of a tender-hearted Jack who left Lowell and lead "a rucksack revolution," the pot-smoking Ti Jean reciting sutras in Berkeley cottages. The Jack whom they would have preferred to get On the Bus ten years later, who would have dropped more acid instead of knocking back boilermakers, who would have listened to rock and roll instead of fuddy-duddy jazz music, who'd have a poster of Che on his wall instead of a painting of the Pope, a smiling dashboard Buddha in place of St. Christopher. There was more than a tad of condescension in their nostalgia for the old Jack, or the Jack that never was, condescension in their lamentations over a pot-bellied Kerouac with a silver dollar taped over his navel hernia, dying in St. Pete clutching his rosary beads. So to his biographers, Jack Kerouac, after the publication of *The Dharma Bums*, ceased to exist.

Jack Kerouac wasn't a rebel, he was a cultural revolutionary. Rebels are committed to what they are rebelling against, want parents or town, country, college, or peers to take notice of them, to shake a finger, acknowledge their rebellion, say the sorries, and accept them back into the fold. Kerouac didn't give a flying fuck about any of that. He changed the way things are by being the way he was. One doesn't salute a tree for spreading its foliage, though some would cut it down.

Kerouac wasn't merely a representative of another culture with a different language — it often seemed as if he were part of another race, or from another planet.

"I was just somebody else," he wrote in *On the Road*, "some stranger, and my whole life was a haunted life, the life of a ghost."

In a very real sense, he didn't belong anywhere. He wasn't really a football player, a workingman, or a literary type, and, ironically, he made the least likely of beatniks. You see him in group photos with the likes of Ginsberg, Corso, Orlovsky, and he is definitely the odd man out. It's as if someone pasted his picture in, like the notorious head of Chairman Mao glued to a lacustrine background for the purpose of proving the man still existed. You could see it was a bad scissors job. With Jack too, one needed proof he was there. And he was, but he also was not there.

At the beginning of *Vanity of Duluoz*, Kerouac mourns the fact that people no longer act the way they used to act. Instead of walking down streets whistling, hands in pockets, they now stride eyes straight ahead, eyes on the main chance, fearful. A North America dominated by the hideous expression "You're putting me on."

He lamented that in the past thirty years people had changed so much he no longer recognized them as people, or himself as "a real member of something called the human race."

In 1965, in a letter to a reader named Raman Singh, Kerouac drew a prescient picture of a future distinguished by "Overpopulation, computers, machine-tooled minds, schoolyard socialism, mechanistic cops, robots, antennae, beeps, creeps."

What unites Kerouac's early detractors and later biographers is their almost total aversion to his Catholicism. But Kerouac's Catholicism, with its imagery, hagiography, mysticism, and promise of the big payoff at the end, is the most important aspect of his work and life. Many Kerouac readers that I know — some of whom have written about him — either shake their heads at the iconographic references or are repulsed by them. Some devotees won't even open a copy of *Visions of Gerard*. Others, when they come across "the Catholic stuff," skip ahead a few pages, as if turning a deaf ear to a loved one's quirk. But there are thousands of such passages in Kerouac's work. They might as well skip his entire output.

I've noticed that many people have a weird, almost reverse-Pavlovian, reaction to Catholic references and iconography. This is comparable to the response that others — and some of the same, no doubt — have to anything referring to what they interpret as Jewishness. These people's prejudice blinds them to the greatness of much of Kerouac's work, particularly the Christian mystic masterpiece, *Visions of Gerard*, just as it might blind them to Allen Ginsberg's mystic long-line incantatory masterpiece, *Kaddish*.

Kerouac would have been more palatable if it weren't for all that stuff about saints. Why does he have to go mention the likes of St. Francis, who they know liked to feed the birds but otherwise see as some old "authority figure" of the church? But Kerouac's St. Francis was the actual visionary who had started out as a playboy, and wrote *The Canticle of the Sun*, and in his last years suffered the pain of his stigmata while waiting on "Lady Death."

When Kerouac meets that old hobo at the beginning of *The Dharma Bums*, many of his readers wished the fellow would have been some wandering Berkeley *bhikkhu* or *Tathagata* tramp rather than an adherent of St. Theresa, who happened to be Kerouac's favorite saint. They might have been open-minded, or open-hearted, enough to learn of St. Theresa's "little way" of trust and love. A "little way" that Kerouac would like to have followed had he not been born a century later than Theresa, and into chaos.

I find it interesting that *The Dharma Bums* is the favorite book of people whose worldview coincides with the ideas rampant in the Sixties. Kerouac's only autobiographical work in which the protagonist has an unambiguously Anglo-Saxon protestant name — Ray Smith — *The Dharma Bums* is his most American novel, Buddhists being much more assimilable than Catholic mystics.

Kerouac's message of tenderness and piety was constant. His belief in God was best expressed in an 1967 interview: "When the hell will people realize that all living beings whether human or animals, whether earthly or from other planets, are representatives of God, and that they should be treated as such, that all things whether living or inanimate and whether alive, dead, or unborn, and whether in the form of matter or empty space, are simply the body of God."

Sometimes he spoke it directly, sometimes he embodied the message in the stories of Christian saints or Bodhisattvas. As Gary Snyder pointed out, Kerouac took immediately to the stories and mythology of Buddhism, particularly the "Four Sights," or what Siddhartha Gautama learned on his first day abroad. He was a pampered young man but finally left the castle grounds in his chariot with his charioteer and saw (1) an old man; he had never seen one before, and he realized aging; (2) sickness, and understood suffering; (3) death, and he knew then the absolute fate of every living thing; (4) over there was a holy man, a *sadhu*, who seemed to be at peace, despite his knowledge of the first three sights. And the sadhu sat under a tree, like Buddha later under the bodhi tree. And because trees are holy — whether simply as living things, or as Buddhist symbolism — two days before he died, Kerouac raged when his next-door neighbor cut down the backyard Georgia pine through whose limbs and needles the wind at night whistled and he watched the stars.

Kerouac's life is so much a classic pilgrimage, and his work a record of that pilgrimage, that it often seems as if he had carefully plotted his road. Or that it was preordained. And during that search, he encountered like-minded souls — a purpose of the classic pilgrimage — and often the views shared by these people conflicted with those of the established church as well as the secular powers. But having encountered like-minded souls, the true pilgrim was, nevertheless, impelled to wander on alone.

Pilgrimages are important to all religions and even have their roots in pre-religious pagan cultures. The typical explanation of the pilgrimage holds that it is a journey by the faithful to a site that is important in the religion — Mecca, Jerusalem — and that there are two parts to this journey, the external moving through space, and the more important internal one, both resulting in renewal or reaffirmation of faith.

But journeys do not need to have a specific site or shrine as their destination to be recognized by the holy as true pilgrimages. Any place will do, or no particular place at all. Once on the road, the holy person can be alone with his thoughts of God.

And then there were the great and daring ventures of the old-time Irish monks who considered the only worthy pilgrimage to be a leap into the unknown. That's why they built those reed boats and cast off at the mercy of God and the elements. (And what we now call North America is the least of what they discovered.)

Thomas Merton, in *Mystics and Zen Masters*, has said that the pilgrimage of the Irish monk was not the "restless search of an unsatisfied romantic heart" but rather a "profound and existential tribute to realities perceived in the very structure of the world." He was constantly in the thrall of bodily and spiritual realities, and struggling with them "resulted in an astounding spiritual creativity which made it impossible for the

Celtic monk merely to accept his existence as something static."

And Merton might have been talking about Kerouac, with whom he corresponded, and who traced his family name back to the Celtic Kerr or Carr, when he wrote that, "his vocation was to mystery and growth, to liberty and to abandonment in God, in self-commitment to apparent irrationality. . . . "

Visualizing those monks of the eighth, ninth, and tenth centuries, called gyrovagues, taking off, wandering the roads, headed for Avignon because there was someone there who had a book that might provide answers, I can't help but think of the first meetings of the searchers who came to be called the Beat Generation. You see the wise older monk, he's been around, wasn't always interested in visions and enlightenment, he's loitering there by the wall of dripping stone and sees his buddies, come from all over, and takes illuminated manuscripts from under his robes to give them. It's like William Burroughs on Times Square, mid-Forties, giving Baudelaire, Céline, Rimbaud's *Illuminations* to Kerouac and Ginsberg.

This sort of thing has always been going on, creating a spiritual continuum across centuries, from gyrovagues to beats. The toughest struggle of all is try and meld the sacred and profane, the natural and supernatural, this world and the next. Admit to this preoccupation and you're in deep trouble with your church and your state. Try to make a record of it, as did St. Augustine, or St. John of the Cross, or William Blake, and you're scorned and, perhaps, imprisoned by your contemporaries, even if later generations regard you — usually without reading you — as a classic. St. Augustine with his wives and concubines; roistering with dissolute friends and worrying about his mother; simultaneously seeking God and lusting. Snatch him out of his time, and transpose him to Crossbay Boulevard, Queens, returning weary to his mother's little apartment after parties in the city, with regrets, hung-over and depressed; how to reconcile sordid practices with glimpses of eternity, "not knowing that great misery was involved in this very thing," writes St. Augustine in his *Confessions*, "that, being thus sunk and blinded, I could not discern that light of excellence and beauty, to be embraced for its own sake, which the eye of the flesh cannot see, and is seen by the inner man. Nor did I, unhappy, consider from what source it sprang, that even on these things, foul as they were, I with pleasure discoursed with my friends, nor could I, even according to the notions I then had of happiness, be happy without my friends, amid what abundance soever of carnal pleasures. And yet these friends I loved for themselves only and I felt that I was beloved of them again for myself only."

I think of all that hysteria over the term "Beat," or "Beat generation"; columnists and TV commentators wanting to believe, or pretending to believe, that it had something to do with beating people up, and Kerouac explaining sincerely that it means being at the bottom of your personality looking up, that it means beatitude and beatific. After two whole years of explaining, there he is on the Ben Hecht TV show, the garrulous old bore greets him, and Kerouac, as if knowing the asininity to follow — as if at dawn the old padre has shown up at his cell to lead him to the Chair, or the Cross — mutters a fatalistic "Hello, Ben."

I've seen all the TV shows, and heard the radio tapes, and read the articles and columns and interviews, and Kerouac's explanation of Beat is always the same, really, though with nuances. I had always wondered at a particular historical explanation, or derivation, of Beat which I thought to be conspicuous by its absence in Kerouac's accounts. Surely, he must have known of that other beat group that preceded his own by nearly four hundred years. Kerouac, who was familiar with the history of Catholicism, who read his St. John of the Cross, and who makes reference to the Children's Crusade and the Spanish Inquisition. St. John of the Cross wrote his "Spiritual Canticle," the great religious poem of his era, under a skylight in a bathroom, just as Jack Kerouac wrote "Mexico City Blues," which Michael McClure and others have called the great religious poem of his era, under a skylight in a bathroom.

Then, listening carefully, for the third or fourth time, to tapes Kerouac made at the Northport library in 1964, I found confirmation that he knew of the centuries-old antecedent of the Beat movement. His friend Stanley Twardowicz and a Hungarian assistant librarian are having their own etymological discussion, Kerouac keeping out of it until finally you hear him, probably out of exasperation, mutter one word, "Beatas!"

The Spanish Inquisition lasted for six hundred years, from the thirteenth to nineteenth centuries, but the suppression of "heresy" was never more intense than in the 1500s. The horror was greatest in Spain with its secret tribunals, the auto-da-fé, and sadistic punishments. Catholics were made to practice a sterile religion for fear of punishment, and it was this situation that John Calvin and Martin Luther protested, and which gave rise within the Catholic Church to a Counter-Reformation. But there was, as well, a sort of crisis cult, or mystical revolt of Catholics. And these people were called the "beatas."

These sixteenth-century Beats believed in piety, tenderness, divine love, and love for all living things, and bowed to no authority's notions of virtue. One historian, Antonio T. de Nicolas, might be lifting a line from Allen Ginsberg's *Howl* when he writes of the earlier Beats, "who talked to everyone, including the Inquisition, of love, ecstasies, erotic visions, and instant salvation."

Kerouac lived the most chaotic of days, but there is an almost classic symmetry to his life and work. In October 1969, it is as if he knew the end had come and he greeted it almost joyously. He drew up a new will, wrote farewell letters, finished a novel, and was by all accounts happy. The wheel of things had made a complete turn and it is as if Jack realized he was about to get that glimpse of heaven.

In his potboiler novel *On the Road*, crossing the continent in 1948, in search of the holy undefinable It, Sal Paradise encountered another pilgrim who bid him to "*Go moan for man.*"

In *Pic*, the novel Kerouac finished a few days before he died, the young black boy and his older brother are leaving New York, bound for the coast that same year of 1948. And there, through the middle of the carnival of Times Square, the tawdry dumbshow symbol of the folly of all human endeavor, comes the same white-haired pilgrim with the same message: *"Go moan for man."*

That old pilgrim was there in all the other books too — he just didn't make himself so obvious. But look again and you can glimpse him in the corner of the wildest parties, or see his shadow in red-brick alleys, spy him in the sideview mirror at dusty crossroads, and notice how in the desert he's a white-robed form always disappearing on the shimmering horizon. That old pilgrim was Jack Kerouac himself — and still is, and, what's more, always will be.

And you hear him murmur as he's passing through, "Go thou unto the earth, go moan for man."

# Appendix

*This essay first appeared in 1979 in a magazine devoted to Kerouaciana called* The Moody Street Irregulars. *Its intention was to say something about Kerouac's much discussed and mostly misunderstood interest in jazz. Kerouac's love of progressive jazz, whether of the Pres or Bird schools, was as alien to the status quo of the Fifties as to the status quo of the Sixties. As well I wished, incidentally, to emphasize the complex of people and ideas, with Kerouac as the matrix.*

## JACK AND JAZZ:
## Woodsmoke and Trains

This is about Jack Kerouac, Brew Moore, and a bass player called Charlie Leeds. It is also about jazz, but, more than anything, it is about an entire way of life that has ceased to exist — just as Jack and Brew and Charlie have ceased to exist — and further, can no longer exist, because the rules have changed and the world has changed.

Much has been made of Jack Kerouac's jazz concerns and the influence it had on his writing. His interest is obvious, from the earliest big-band reviews for the Horace Mann literary magazine to his statement to a friend in Tampa in 1968 that "I got every record Charlie Parker ever made." But the stylistic influence is obscured by a lot of misunderstanding.

Those frantic, frenetic, and we can't leave out peripatetic, post-war years were the same years that the jazz revolution, known as bop, was let loose on the land at large, and Kerouac wrote of those "children of the bop American night." But he also wrote, in *On the Road*, of Slam Steward, Lennie Tristano, George Shearing, Billie Holiday, and a guy called Lampshade sweating the blues in a North Beach club. None of this was bebop, but the critics saddled Kerouac with the tag. Anything that you couldn't fox-trot to, like Glen Gray, was labeled as the new bebop. Jack's writing made no sense and jazz made no sense, so, therefore . . .

It happened along about 1940 that young scattered musicians were beginning to do funny, weird, and dissonant things for reasons known only to themselves. A drummer named Kenny Clarke redirected the beat from the bass drum to the top cymbal to produce subtle yet fragmented rhythms. Dizzy Gillespie turned off the Roy Eldridge main trumpet road into an unmapped area of advanced harmonics. And one night in a Harlem chili house, Charlie Parker started to use, as a melody line, the higher intervals of a particular chord, and, with suitable and connected changes, began to play what he had been hearing since the days spent hanging around outside of Twelfth Street clubs in old Kansas City, Missouri.

Here is a connection: In 1941, Dizzy Gillespie made a recording with a guy named Jerry Newman. It was a tune based on the changes of "Exactly Like You," but they couldn't call it that without paying royalties. Newman suggested they give it the name of a friend of his, and Dizzy agreed. The tune offers the first recorded evidence of a procedure that became characteristic of bop. Dizzy slipped into chords with notes half a step away from the expected ones. He played off the beat. The tune is called "Kerouac."

Jack listened and dug, but he didn't borrow. His main love was an older music: swing. His prose had the texture of the ensembles that were the basis of swing music. And when he let loose with one of his pages-long improvisations, it was like a tenor man stepping out of a section and blowing chorus after rolling chorus.

But most significantly, Kerouac never made a mere show of his technique and virtuosity. The story was the important thing. In bebop, the melody is implicit but not stated. If you know the changes, you can infer what the tune is based on. In swing, the melody — that is, the story — is always there.

In his *Paris Review* interview, Kerouac says, "In poetry, you can be completely free to say anything you want, you don't have to tell a story." But prose is a different matter: "I always say, 'No time for poetry now, get your plain tale.'"

Thus it is natural that his favorite jazz musician was the beautiful tenor storyteller Lester Young, "that gloomy saintly goof in whom the history of jazz is wrapped."

Charlie Parker was a shouting congregation in a sweaty clapboard church; a raw, blustering lover; a train in the night rushing double-time and never looking back.

Lester Young was woodsmoke on an autumn morning. He always sounded as if he was standing at the very edge of the world and remembering everything that was good and everything that broke his heart, and was blowing it all out into the great void.

And, of course, Jack was like that.

Jazz musicians coming of age in that time had to choose between Charlie Parker and Lester Young. The greatest of Pres's disciples was Brew Moore, who was known to say: "Anybody who doesn't play like Pres is wrong."

Brew Moore was born in a small town that he always returned to: Indianola, Mississippi. He quit Ol Miss in Faulkner's Oxford and gigged in Memphis before drifting down to New Orleans and Bourbon Street clubs. "I played in so many strip joints," Brew recalled, "I was twenty-one years old before I ever saw a naked woman from the front."

Brew hit New York in 1947 with the Claude Thornhill band. It was on Fifty-Second Street that he saw and dug the bass player Charlie Leeds, who was working in a combo with vibraphonist Terry Gibbs. Charlie and Brew became best friends in those days, as Charlie and I would be best friends in later years. He used to talk about all that: those years just after the war when they had returned to a new America and a world come apart. America had obliterated entire cities in the name of peace and progress. Part of a generation rushed hell-bent for fresh subdivisions and, for the first time in history, the other part rushed in the opposite direction. The rug had been yanked from underneath. For people like Charlie and Brew, music made sense.

## The Long Slow Death of Jack Kerouac 101

If they could learn to play beautifully, then everything would work out. There would be rhyme and a reason. Well, they did learn to play — they were among the best of their time — but, of course, no secrets were revealed. The world was as cockeyed as ever.

Charlie and Brew had this outlook in common as well as a preference for the lag-along playing style of Lester Young. Also, unlike that of most jazzmen of the era, their creative interests were not limited to music. Brew wrote tortured, introspective poems; Charlie was a painter and sculptor and had even formed an artists' band, with his friend Larry Rivers playing baritone sax. Rivers, who was to do the illustrations for *Lonesome Traveler*, introduced Charlie to Kerouac in the White Rose Bar.

Brew and Charlie played and recorded with the best groups of their time, but on the spur of the moment — usually high or juiced — were liable to quit and dash across the country, maybe to gig with country bands in the South or to join obscure jazz combos in Detroit neighborhood bars.

But the music scene extracted its dues. Both were disillusioned with the music business, not to mention the business of the world. Brew and Charlie were both strung out by then, and finally Charlie just quit the New York scene. "We had an apartment together on Ninety-Ninth Street," Charlie told me. "Brew was trying to kick, but he couldn't. One day in May of 1949, he'd had a recording date the night before and had gotten so juiced he fell out in the street and somebody copped his horn. The next morning I remember saying to Brew, 'Are you still going to try to kick your thing or not?' He said, 'Man, I don't know *what* I'm going to do.' And I said, 'Well, I can't make any of this anymore.' And I left and never went back. I never saw Brew again."

Brew Moore was sitting on a bench in Washington Square fingering his tenor when a way out of his dilemma presented itself in the form of a 1949 Buick convertible. The driver was a guy called Billy Faier, who shouted, "Anyone for the coast?"

Brew thought, "Why not?" and jumped in. There were two other passengers: Ramblin' Jack Elliot and Woody Guthrie. Things proceeded smoothly until Texas, when Faier suggested stopping and playing a little music. Brew said their kinds of music didn't mix, but Faier swore he could play some blues. Brew agreed on the condition that he could wet his chops with some wine. So the two of them sat beside the road blowing, and Woody Guthrie sat in the car fuming. Eyeing the wine, but fuming all the same. He hated jazz and wouldn't talk to Brew the rest of the trip.

"But we were the only juiceheads in the car," Brew remembered. "So Woody would say to Jack or Billy: 'Would you ask Brew if he'd like to split a bottle of port with me?' And I'd say: 'That's cool, Woody.' But he wouldn't answer. All the way to the coast like that."

Brew gigged in California, cut some records, and, at one point, got together with Kenneth Rexroth for a jazz-and-poetry date. He was working the Cellar the day Kerouac came in and saw him, "his cheeks distended in a round ball . . . and he plays perfect harmony to any tune they bring up. . . . He pays little attention to anyone, he drinks his beer, he gets loaded and eye-heavy, but he never misses a beat or a note, because music is his heart, and in music he has found that pure message to give to the world — only trouble is they don't understand."

And not long thereafter sweet jazz died in America and was replaced by the discordant and mean sounds of something called *free jazz*. The music turned its back on the audience. Brew went to Europe — spent the Sixties and early Seventies in Paris and Copenhagen, scuffling. There wasn't that much work over there for a white jazz musician. The clubs wanted black Americans first, but at least there were enough jobs to scrape by. Occasionally a serious and intent young European would ask for his autograph: "Excuse me, aren't you the hepcat Jack Kerouac wrote about?"

Throughout the years, Brew exchanged letters with Charlie Leeds and made plans and drank. He was drunk the day he died. As Charlie wrote to me when he found out in 1973: "Brew fell down a Danish staircase into the biggest bunch of nothing you ever saw."

> I'm sitting there on the edge of the bandstand right at Brew's feet.... Brew is blowing ... "Birth of the Blues," down jazzy, and when his turn comes to enter he comes up with a perfect beautiful new idea that announces the glory of the future world.... I tap him on the shoe-top to acknowledge he's right — In between sets he sits beside me and Gia and doesn't say much and appears to pretend not to be able to say much — He'll say it on his horn. —

Jack drank himself to death and so did Brew. Ironically, Charlie Leeds, who had been a junkie for thirty years, got too old and beat to score and had to turn to the sauce till it got him too. Now they are all dead and gone. Gone like that music and that age.

> Heaven's time-worm eats at Brew's vitals as mine, as yours, it's hard enough to live in a world where you grow old and die, why be disharmonious?

"The old gravedigger picks up his shovel and closes the book."

— Jack Kerouac, *Visions of Gerard*

# Afterword

The previous pages are not the completion of any writing assignment — a job of work — but are, rather, the result of more than thirty-five years of reading Jack Kerouac, and reading about Jack Kerouac. I have read in other fields too. Unlike, it seems, many other commentators. Also, thank God, I had some social, political and literary consciousness before the summer of 1967. So the opinions expressed are entirely my own.

But when I put an opinion in someone else's mouth, I either read it somewhere or that person told it to me personally. I didn't go out to interview anyone, but had occasion, over the last few decades, to converse with people who knew Jack Kerouac or had some connection to the Beat Generation. And, yes, I met and talked with Allen Ginsberg. Hell, it would probably be difficult to find someone who *hasn't* talked to Ginsberg. But, more importantly, I am proud to have been, for twenty years, a friend of the incomparable John Montgomery, a buddy of Jack's and a character in three of his novels. A weird satirist of the whole scene, Kerouac called him. John once hired Jack to dig out a basement on a house he intended to renovate. John once hired me to dig a trench around a house he intended to renovate. We have that in common. John was not even remotely like any other human I've ever encountered and, quite frankly, the man was nuts. Kerouac describes him exactly as he was.

I talked about JK with musicians: Graham Cournoyer (also known as McKeen), David Amram, Helen Humes, and Al Cohn — who told me that Kerouac played piano on some of the sessions that were released as *Blues and Haikus*; I discussed JK with Ted Joans outside Shakespeare and Company in Paris. I've talked telephonically with wives one and three — Edie and Stella. I've benefited from Stan Twardowicz's insights in letters and run up the phone bill with Cliff Anderson.

Once in a jazz club in Toronto, I spoke to the great saxophonist Zoot Sims who, with Al Cohn, was part of that *Blues and Haikus* date. Sims, a serious boozer in his own right, insisted he'd never had anything to do with any such recording project and had never heard of anyone called Jack Kerouac.

I never spoke or corresponded with Brew Moore but he knew that I admired his music — having been told by my friend Charlie Leeds. Brew would occasionally pass along comments to Charlie for relay to me. One was: Anyone who doesn't play like Pres is wrong. And I was touched, more than I can say, when not long before Brew died, he sent a package of his own writings as well as photographs of a young himself and friends, many of them soon-to-be-famous musicians, to Charlie to give to me.

Back in New York City in 1968, on a stairway between the second and third floors at 86 Eldridge Street near Grand and Bowery, a handsome black-haired guy in a black leather jacket who looked like a thief hit me up for a buck. He was going down and I was going up.

# The Long Slow Death of Jack Kerouac 109

When I got up to the third floor, I asked my friend who the guy was. That's Herbert Huncke, Bruce Elwell said. Jack Kerouac must have been a saint to find anything good to say about that guy. I had a room in that apartment in an old-fashioned Manhattan tenement with the tub in the kitchen and the toilets in the hall. One morning, when I went out to the hall, I discovered a guy with a mane of red hair, on his knees, scrubbing the floor around the toilet. "Hi," he said, "I'm Peter Orlovsky." And he was. Who would kid about a thing like that? I ran into him often, and there was usually an army gas-mask bag filled with cleaning products hanging from his shoulder. Once I helped him move out of an apartment. I think he was on the outs with Allen. There was another fellow involved, and from one trunk could be seen bits of women's apparel.

Then there was Adam Ydobon of San Francisco whom I met in 1978 at the annual hobo convention in Britt, Iowa, where he was politicking to be crowned King of the Hoboes. Adam, born in China during the Boxer Rebellion, had been defeated in his last outing, the '76 presidential go, by Jimmy Carter (whose most recent biographer, Douglas Brinkley, has been hand-picked by the Sampas clan to tell the Jack Kerouac tale yet again). This time, sources — reliable sources — claim, a great love affair between the author and Stella. Anyway, Adam's campaign slogan had been Nobody For President. Nobody being his last name spelled backward. What this has to do with Jack Kerouac is that he and the would-be president/would-be hobo king had been drinking buddies under the bridges and down the alleys of San Francisco. "Jack was going to write a novel about me," Adam said. Before I could reply to the effect that Kerouac said much the same to everyone, Adam added, "But he never lived to finish the thing." — "Finish?" sez I. "Yeah, he got near a hundred pages into it, though." "You ever see the pages?" "Sure, I got a copy of the manuscript at home in my hotel room." "Can I look at them someday?" "Sure, kid. Next time you're in town, I'll show you the whole thing. But I got a couple pages with me now. You want to see them?" Do I? Was Jack Kerouac Catholic?

He showed me a page and three-quarters. The typing resembled that of pages of JK manuscript I'd seen. As for the writing — well, it sure as hell wasn't Truman Capote. You can love or hate Jack Kerouac as much as you please but you can't write like him. It was the real Ti-Jean.

# *Acknowledgments*

*Chapter 3*
Father Armand Morisette, "A Catholic's View of Kerouac," in *Kerouac at the Wild Boar* (Pelo and Fern Press, 1984); Edie Parker's unpublished memoirs; Allen Ginsberg's oft-repeated remarks are from an interview; Marie Livornese, "My Prom Date" in *Newsday*, April 1, 1990; quotations from LuAnne Henderson come from conversations with the author.

*Chapter 5*
Joyce Johnson, *Minor Characters* (Houghton Mifflin, 1983); Walter Gutman, "My Memories of Jack Kerouac," *Limberlost Review*, reprinted in *Kerouac at the Wild Boar*; quotations from Graham Cournoyer and Cliff Anderson come from conversations with the author; Carl Adkins, "Jack Kerouac Off the Road for Good," *The Yearbook of Discovery* (Scholastic Magazine, 1971); Larry Vickers, "Jack Kerouac: End of the Road," *Father Joe's Handy Homilies*, June 1970; Nick Lowe, "Jack Kerouac's St. Petersburg Sojourn," *St. Petersburg Times*, June 7, 1992; quotations from Stella are from an unreleased audiotape with Stella and Danny Desole, December 1969; Jack McClintock, *St. Petersburg Times*, October 12, 1969.

*Chapter 6*
Quotes from Jack Kerouac come from "Last Word" in *Escapade*, March 1958; "The Art of Fiction XLI: Jack Kerouac," *Paris Review*, summer 1968; Allen Ginsberg quoting Norman Podhoretz in a paper presented at the International Jack Kerouac Gathering, October 1987, Quebec City; from Thomas Merton, *Mystics and Zen Masters* (Farrar, Strauss and Giroux, 1967).